Thomas Beer

Design and Implementation of Context-Aware Information Push Systems

Thomas Beer

Design and Implementation of Context-Aware Information Push Systems

A framework for rapidly creating proactive, context-aware, and configurable information systems.

Südwestdeutscher Verlag für Hochschulschriften

Impressum/Imprint (nur für Deutschland/ only for Germany)
Bibliografische Information der Deutschen Nationalbibliothek: Die Deutsche Nationalbibliothek verzeichnet diese Publikation in der Deutschen Nationalbibliografie; detaillierte bibliografische Daten sind im Internet über http://dnb.d-nb.de abrufbar.
 Alle in diesem Buch genannten Marken und Produktnamen unterliegen warenzeichen-, marken- oder patentrechtlichem Schutz bzw. sind Warenzeichen oder eingetragene Warenzeichen der jeweiligen Inhaber. Die Wiedergabe von Marken, Produktnamen, Gebrauchsnamen, Handelsnamen, Warenbezeichnungen u.s.w. in diesem Werk berechtigt auch ohne besondere Kennzeichnung nicht zu der Annahme, dass solche Namen im Sinne der Warenzeichen- und Markenschutzgesetzgebung als frei zu betrachten wären und daher von jedermann benutzt werden dürften.

Verlag: Südwestdeutscher Verlag für Hochschulschriften Aktiengesellschaft & Co. KG
Dudweiler Landstr. 99, 66123 Saarbrücken, Deutschland
Telefon +49 681 37 20 271-1, Telefax +49 681 37 20 271-0
Email: info@svh-verlag.de
Zugl.: Innsbruck, University of Innsbruck, Dissertation, 2009

Herstellung in Deutschland:
Schaltungsdienst Lange o.H.G., Berlin
Books on Demand GmbH, Norderstedt
Reha GmbH, Saarbrücken
Amazon Distribution GmbH, Leipzig
ISBN: 978-3-8381-0012-8

Imprint (only for USA, GB)
Bibliographic information published by the Deutsche Nationalbibliothek: The Deutsche Nationalbibliothek lists this publication in the Deutsche Nationalbibliografie; detailed bibliographic data are available in the Internet at http://dnb.d-nb.de.
 Any brand names and product names mentioned in this book are subject to trademark, brand or patent protection and are trademarks or registered trademarks of their respective holders. The use of brand names, product names, common names, trade names, product descriptions etc. even without a particular marking in this works is in no way to be construed to mean that such names may be regarded as unrestricted in respect of trademark and brand protection legislation and could thus be used by anyone.

Publisher: Südwestdeutscher Verlag für Hochschulschriften Aktiengesellschaft & Co. KG
Dudweiler Landstr. 99, 66123 Saarbrücken, Germany
Phone +49 681 37 20 271-1, Fax +49 681 37 20 271-0
Email: info@svh-verlag.de

Printed in the U.S.A.
Printed in the U.K. by (see last page)
ISBN: 978-3-8381-0012-8

Copyright © 2010 by the author and Südwestdeutscher Verlag für Hochschulschriften Aktiengesellschaft & Co. KG and licensors
All rights reserved. Saarbrücken 2010

Note

In an effort to maintain consistency and clarity this thesis has been written using a masculine gender. However, this is not intended, nor should imply any gender prejudice.

Abstract

The novel class of *context-aware information push systems* (CAIPS) aims – like ubiquitous computing systems – to provide the right information for the right person at the right time and the right place; such systems provide their users automatically with tailored information consequently reducing their search and complexity costs. One of the key enablers of these systems is context-awareness; context-aware systems tailor services and information to their users exploiting information about the users' current situation. Traditional context-aware systems are focused on environmental and computing context information such as the user's location, the current weather, or the current display resolution of the employed mobile device. CAIPS, however, as proposed in this thesis also incorporates the user's preferences regarding products (i.e., information) they might be interested in.

This thesis proposes a conceptual framework facilitating the rapid development of context-aware information push systems; this framework serves as a comprehensive guideline by providing a *reference model* and a *rule language framework*. The former defines the fundamental functional and logical parts of CAIPS; the latter supports the development of specific reactive rule languages. Such a rule language is employed to declaratively specify the automatic sending of tailored messages to the users, i.e., to declaratively define *what* should be sent to *whom* and *when*. The development of new applications compliant to this framework ensures that the requirements posed by context-aware information push systems are met. The framework itself is developed based on a thorough examination of the following techniques:

- Context-Aware Systems
- Knowledge Representation & Expert Systems
- Publish/Subscribe Systems
- Recommender Systems

The thesis shows that the methodical synthesis of these techniques perfectly tackles the requirements posed by CAIPS. A case study on the design and implementation of a specific CAIPS, drawing on the mobile tourist guide *innsbruck.mobile*, proves the applicability of the proposed conceptual framework. This implementation serves as the basis for a detailed, qualitative evaluation.

Acknowledgements

I would like to thank all those who have offered me their support and encouragement throughout the PhD trajectory.

First and foremost, I would like to thank my supervisor Professor Hannes Werthner for supporting this thesis with his beneficial ideas and constructive criticism. Also, I would like to thank Professor Dieter Fensel for taking over the part of the second referee.

Many people provided feedback to early drafts of this thesis. I would like to thank particularly Dr. Gordon Fraser, Dr. Markus Zanker, and Jörg Rasinger for thoughtful contribution and criticism. For further assistance I would like to kindly thank Stefanie Lindner, Owen McCormack, and Kathrin Fleckl.

I am honored to have Professor Hannes Werthner, Professor Dieter Fensel, and Professor Aart Middeldorp as members of my PhD committee. I thank each one of them for accepting the invitation.

I would like to thank the CEOs of the eTourism Competence Center Austria Dr. Wolfram Höpken and Dr. Matthias Fuchs for giving me the opportunity to participate in the ECCA team during my research. For the numerous inspiring discussions (also in the off-office life) I especially would like to thank Jörg Rasinger. In addition, I would like to thank Friedrich Gustav Wachter whose bachelor thesis has contributed to my work. For supporting me in implementational issues a special thank you goes to Markus Jessenitschnig. For inspiring discussions concerning location-based services I would like to thank Robert Walter and Christian Vogt.

Finally, I would like to thank my family and my friends for supporting and encouraging me during all the time of this work. I particularly would like to thank my parents Elisabeth and Hans for believing in and supporting me.

2008 was a hard year for me. Therefore, last but not least I would like to thank E. O., the person who encouraged me to go on. To her I dedicate not only this thesis, but also my heart.

Contents

1 Introduction 1
   1.1 Motivation 2
      1.1.1 Study: Behavioral Intention to Use 3
         1.1.1.1 Study design 3
         1.1.1.2 Study results 4
      1.1.2 Example Message Types 7
   1.2 Objectives of CAIPS 8
   1.3 Contribution 9
   1.4 Thesis Outline 10
2 Background and Theoretical Foundations 12
   2.1 Knowledge Representation and Expert Systems 12
      2.1.1 Knowledge Representation 13
      2.1.2 Knowledge Representation Technologies 18
         2.1.2.1 Object-Oriented Representation Technology 18
         2.1.2.2 Rules 19
         2.1.2.3 Ontologies 20
      2.1.3 Expert Systems 21
         2.1.3.1 Demarcation of Expert Systems 24
      2.1.4 Utilization within CAIPS & Discussion 26
   2.2 Context-Aware Systems 27
      2.2.1 Basics 27
      2.2.2 Architecture 32
      2.2.3 Utilization within CAIPS & Discussion 34
   2.3 Publish/Subscribe Systems 34
      2.3.1 Terminology of Publish/Subscribe Systems 35
      2.3.2 Structure 36
         2.3.2.1 Events and Notifications 36
         2.3.2.2 Producers and Consumers 37
         2.3.2.3 Subscriptions 38
         2.3.2.4 Event Notification Service 40

	2.3.3	Models of Interaction & Abstraction Levels	40
	2.3.4	Subscription Language & Event Algebra	43
	2.3.5	Utilization within CAIPS & Discussion	45
2.4		Recommender Systems	46
	2.4.1	Utilization within CAIPS & Discussion	50
3	Designing CAIPS		52
3.1		Overview of CAIPS	52
3.2		Stakeholders	56
3.3		Requirements Elicitation	56
3.4		Definitions	58
	3.4.1	Message Type	58
	3.4.2	Information Value Chain Concept	58
	3.4.3	Information Value Chain Instance	59
	3.4.4	Message Instance	59
	3.4.5	Final Message	60
	3.4.6	Message Triggering Situation	61
	3.4.7	Duplicate Message	61
3.5		Conceptual Framework	61
	3.5.1	Reference Model	62
	3.5.1.1	Knowledge-Base	64
	3.5.1.2	Rule Interpreter	65
	3.5.1.3	IVCI Retrieval	66
	3.5.1.4	Explanation Provider	66
	3.5.1.5	Publisher	67
	3.5.1.6	Event Service	67
	3.5.1.7	Context Provider	68
	3.5.1.8	Sensor	68
	3.5.1.9	Message Renderer	68
	3.5.1.10	Message Gateway	68
	3.5.1.11	IVCI Provider	68
	3.5.1.12	Add-On Services	69
	3.5.1.13	User Interfaces	69
	3.5.2	Context-Aware Information Triggering Language (CAITL)	70
	3.5.2.1	Combining Knowledge Representations	70
	3.5.2.2	CAITL: Modular Framework	71

	3.5.2.3	CAITL: Global Semantics ... 72
	3.5.2.4	CAITL: Syntax ... 75
	3.5.2.5	CAITL: Communication and Built-In Variables ... 79
	3.5.2.6	CAITL: Rule Execution Example ... 85

4 Case Study: innsbruck.mobile ... 91
   4.1 CAIPS-IM: Context Representation ... 92
   4.2 CAIPS-IM: CAITL-IM ... 95
      4.2.1 CAITL-IM: Applied Message Types & Corresponding Rules ... 98
   4.3 CAIPS-IM: Architecture ... 100
      4.3.1 innsbruck.mobile – System Overview ... 101
         4.3.1.1 CWA Subsystem ... 102
      4.3.2 CAIPS-IM – Conceptual View ... 104
         4.3.2.1 PushServer ... 104
         4.3.2.2 MessagingServiceClient ... 110
      4.3.3 Innsbruck.mobile – Deployment View ... 110
   4.4 Qualitative Evaluation ... 113
      4.4.1 Service Provider Requirements ... 113
         4.4.1.1 Automatic Message Delivery ... 113
         4.4.1.2 Situation Dependent Message Content Definition ... 114
         4.4.1.3 Automatic Personalization ... 114
         4.4.1.4 Extensibility ... 114
         4.4.1.5 Ease-of-Use ... 114
         4.4.1.6 Multiple Communication Channels ... 119
      4.4.2 User Requirements ... 119
         4.4.2.1 Expressive Subscription Specification ... 119
         4.4.2.2 Practical Subscription Interfaces ... 121
         4.4.2.3 Avoid Similar Message Content ... 121

5 Related Work ... 123
   5.1 SOCAM ... 123
      5.1.1 Overview ... 123
      5.1.2 Discussion ... 124
   5.2 SE Framework for Context-Aware Pervasive Computing ... 125
      5.2.1 Overview ... 125
      5.2.2 Discussion ... 126
   5.3 CybreMinder ... 127

	5.3.1	Overview	127
	5.3.2	Discussion	128
	5.4	COMPASS	129
	5.4.1	Overview	129
	5.4.2	Discussion	129
	5.5	Summary	130
6	Conclusion		133
	6.1	Summary	133
	6.2	Future Work	135

List of Figures

Figure 1: Data - Information - Knowledge 13
Figure 2: Rule Types 19
Figure 3: Expert System Overview 23
Figure 4: Publish/Subscribe System 36
Figure 5: subject-based subscription 39
Figure 6: Non-Personalized Recommender System 46
Figure 7: Content-Based Recommendation Strategy 48
Figure 8: Collaborative Recommendation Strategy 49
Figure 9: Collaborative Filtering, Example 49
Figure 10: Demographic Based Collaborative Filtering 50
Figure 11: Overview Context-Aware Information Delivery 54
Figure 12: Message Type 58
Figure 13: Message Type Body 58
Figure 14: Design of Message Instance 60
Figure 15: Message Type, Message Instance, Final Message 60
Figure 16: 1 Message Type – n Message Instances – n Final Messages 61
Figure 17: CAIPS – Reference Model 63
Figure 18: Context and IVCI Data 64
Figure 19: CAITL Rule Parts 72
Figure 20: CAITL Rule Definition & Execution 74
Figure 21: CAITL Rule – XML Representation 76
Figure 22: CAITL Syntax – XML Schema Definition 78
Figure 23: Communication Variables – Event Representation Format 80
Figure 24: Representation of a Blizzard Subscription 81
Figure 25: Event Representation Structure– XML Schema Definition 81
Figure 26: Communication Variables – User Representation Format 82
Figure 27: Representation of a User Binding 82
Figure 28: User Representation Structure – XML Schema Definition 83
Figure 29: Communication Variable, Example 84
Figure 30: Blizzard Notification 85

Figure 31: Blizzard Rule – Event Part 85

Figure 32: Blizzard Rule – Subscription Representation 86

Figure 33: Blizzard Rule – Condition Part 86

Figure 34: Blizzard Rule – User Representation 87

Figure 35: Blizzard Rule – Action Part 88

Figure 36: Binding of the Communication Variables 89

Figure 37: Relating CAIPS, CAIPS-IM, etPlanner, and innsbruck.mobile 91

Figure 38: User-Centric Context Representation 92

Figure 39: Contextual Information, Conceptual Representation 94

Figure 40: XML Schema imobile_sl 1.3 96

Figure 41: Example imobile_sl 96

Figure 42: XML Schema – CWA-CL 97

Figure 43: CWA-CL Example 98

Figure 44: innsbruck.mobile System Overview 101

Figure 45: CWA – Specification of Recommendation Rules 103

Figure 46: innsbruck.mobile –Basic Building Blocks of CAIPS-IM 104

Figure 47: PushServer 105

Figure 48: EventGenerator 106

Figure 49: Creating an EventGenerator 106

Figure 50: RuleEngine 108

Figure 51: ActionHandler 109

Figure 52: Message Creation Process 109

Figure 53: Deployment Diagram *innsbruck.mobile* 111

Figure 54: Rule Creation – General Information 115

Figure 55: Rule Creation – Publisher & Corresponding Subscription Creation 116

Figure 56: Rule Creation – Condition Part 117

Figure 57: Rule Creation – Action Part (IVCCs) 118

Figure 58: Rule Creation – Action Part (Template) 119

Figure 59: Information Needs – Type Subscription 120

Figure 60: Information Needs – Preferences Elicitation 120

List of Tables

Table 1: Use-Intention of Mobile Information Services 6
Table 2: Information Services 7
Table 3: Requested Message Types 7
Table 4: Objectives Classified by Involved Stakeholders 8
Table 5: Layers of a Context-Aware System 34
Table 6: Interaction Models 40
Table 7: Context Categories as Employed in CAIPS-IM 93
Table 8: Related Work – Overview 131

1 Introduction

The beginning is the most important part of the work

Plato (427 - 347 BC)

Modern communication systems enable information access at *any time* and *any location*. The phrase *any service for any person any time any where* was coined by research in mobile computing in the early 90's. Significant challenges arising from this are how to deal with information overload and information retrieval effort. Novel information systems are required to tackle these challenges. This can be reached by providing systems which automatically supply their users with exactly that information they are currently interested in. Ubiquitous computing systems (Weiser, 1991), which represent the next step in the evolution chain of distributed systems, aim to tackle these challenges by providing *the right service for the right person at the right time at the right place* (Strang, 2003).

Similarly, *context-aware information push systems* (CAIPS) enable their operators to provide the consumers automatically with tailored messages related to their current situation. Within this thesis the term CAIPS denotes a system type and not a specific implementation, i.e., a family of systems which aim to enable their operators to declaratively specify the proactive sending of tailored messages to his consumers.

The ambitious vision of ubiquitous computing is the design of disappearing computer systems by the invisible integration of computing hardware into everyday environments and artifacts (Weiser, 1991). From a technical perspective ubiquitous computing is characterized by the employment of:

- ad-hoc networks
- smart devices
- context-awareness

Context-awareness is a fundamental for designing ubiquitous computing systems. CAIPS is focused on declarative, context-aware, and mobile information delivery; therefore, CAIPS should rather be considered as a context-aware system than as a ubiquitous computing system.

Subsequently, CAIPS is introduced drawing on a usage scenario from the tourism domain. The rationale behind CAIPS is explained based on both a study determining the attitude of potential end-users towards such a system (cf. Section 1.1.1) and application scenarios from tourism (cf. Section 1.1.2).

1.1 Motivation

The following scenario illustrates the potential benefits of CAIPS in the tourism domain. The scenario focuses on the tourist's perspective and assumes the operation of a CAIPS as an integrated part of a mobile tourist information system (such as *innsbruck.mobile*, cf. Section 4):

> A tourist plans to spend a weekend in Innsbruck/Austria. It is assumed that he has already used the tourist information system during his trip to Vienna/Austria three month ago. Therefore he is already known to the system by means of a user profile (storing both, the users preferences regarding tourism services and the messages he wants to receive). He had stayed in Vienna for two days and, among other things, had visited *Schönbrunn Palace*. Two weeks before departure he interacts with the system to plan his trip to Innsbruck and to complete his user profile with the necessary information for the specified region, e.g., information on activities he is planning to conduct. He loves skiing and therefore searches skiing-regions near Innsbruck. The *Axamer Lizum* seems convincing and he therefore schedules the activity *Skiing in the Axamer Lizum* on Saturday. Two weeks later, on Friday night, he arrives in Innsbruck. During the night there is a spontaneous and disadvantageous weather change - strong wind comes up and updated weather forecasts predict heavy snowfall. At breakfast time a message is sent to his mobile device that there will be a blizzard in *Axamer Lizum* and it is not recommendable to go skiing on that day. Moreover, the message includes a number of alternative suggestions for bad weather activities based on his user profile. Amongst them, the user is welcomed to visit the *Hofburg* in Innsbruck (because he has shown interest in similar historical buildings in the past) and at the same time a 10% rebate on the entry fee is offered. After his visit of the *Hofburg* the system pushes a SMS to his mobile device informing him that *Pizza Gino* offers a special lunch menu (20% off) for all visitors of the *Hofburg* (because the tourist's preferred cuisine is Italian). Both push messages (recommending a visit of the imperial *Hofburg* as a result of the disadvantageous weather change as well as the recommendation of the Italian cuisine after visiting the imperial building) were automatically sent by the CAIPS.
>
> The messages have previously been created by tourism experts from the city of Innsbruck employing the CAIPS. The experts create the messages by specifying situations whose occurrence triggers the delivery of specific information regarding tourism services (specified

1.1 Motivation

by the experts as well). Subsequent to this creation the messages are automatically integrated into the overall system and tourists' may subscribe for these.

Prior to the design of CAIPS a study determining the users' attitude towards such a system was conducted. This study additionally contributes to the rationale for building CAIPS as it shows that enhancing mobile systems with context-aware push functionality significantly improves the acceptance rate of such systems. The study is presented in the subsequent section.

1.1.1 Study: Behavioral Intention to Use

Within this study a survey analyzing the attitude towards such a system and the expected behavioral intention of potential users is presented.

Before presenting the empirical results the most promising functionalities of mobile information systems as suggested in the literature are sketched. In particular, for tourism related mobile information services the latter can be described as search & browse functionalities (Gretzel & Wöber, 2004), value adding functionalities such as context-aware push and recommendation functionalities (Staab & Werthner, 2002; O'Grady & O'Hare, 2002), mCommerce functionalities (e.g. reservation, booking, ticketing, paying, etc.) as well as feedback functionalities (Forum, 2005). The aim of the briefly presented study was to examine whether specific information services such as pushing information about sightseeing influences the perceived acceptance of the entire mobile service. In addition, the particular significance of the above stated functionalities has been evaluated by potential end users, i.e., tourists.

1.1.1.1 Study design

The first determination of potentially successful information services was derived from questions typically posed by tourists at prominent information points within a destination (e.g. tourist information points, welcome centers, taxi, airport, etc.). Thus, 15 qualitative interviews have been conducted in Innsbruck/Austria during September 2005 (Rasinger et al., 2006). Doing so, a total of 290 typical information requests along the destination value-chain could be identified (Bieger, 2005). In addition, focus interviews took place in fall 2005 with 17 individuals from different European countries, i.e., Italy, Germany, and Austria.

The obtained results led to a list comprising a total of 15 potentially successful mobile information services to be used by tourists during destination stay. Described by their functionalities and usability potentials they were evaluated in Tyrol (Austria) in fall 2005 by tourists on the base of a quantitative pilot-study (N = 100) (Rasinger et al., 2006) The top ranked mobile information services were: (1) Transport & navigation, (2) security assistant, (3) news & weather, (4) event information, (5) gastronomy & night-life and (6) sightseeing & shopping. On base of these results a second quantitative study was conducted focusing only on the top six services. For this, in January 2006 a total of 705 tourists was interviewed with respect to their behavioral intentions to use various functionalities of mobile information services. More precise, according to the Technology Acceptance Model (TAM) (F. D. Davis, 1989) the 'intention to use' a specific mobile information service acted as dependent variable whereas the 'intention to use' the various functionalities served as independent variables (Venkatesh et al., 2003). Agreement measurement took place on a 6-point Likert scale. Subsequently, the results of this second study are presented.

1.1.1.2 Study results

The average age of the participants was 33.6 years with a range from 9 to 64 years, 40% were female and 60% male. The majority (i.e., 92%) of the respondents declared skiing and other sports activities as the main purpose of their current destination stay, 3% were present for business reasons. 40% of the respondents were holding a high school-, 32% a college-, and 28% a university degree. 54.9% of the respondents visited Tyrol for 3 days or less and 21.2% booked at least one tourism service via the internet. Generally spoken, the results of the pilot-study (N= 100) have been confirmed as the same mobile information services proved to be attractive for destination usage.

The following paragraph presents the obtained regression results for each of the six examined mobile information services with specific consideration of the *context-aware push* functionality.

1.1 Motivation

Information services	Functionalities	Beta	Description
1. Transport & Navigation	Search & Browse	.203**	Route and transport mean, actual and target position
	Recommendation	n.s.	
	Context-aware P.	.276**	Event-based (e.g. congestion) actively proposes routes
	mCommerce	.161*	Ticketing and reservation for public transport
	Feedback	n.s.	
F-value: 72.87 Sig. of F = .001 Adj. R² = .41			
2. Security Assistant	Search & Browse	.360**	Search for risks per region and tourism activity
	Recommendation	n.s.	
	Context-aware P.	.442**	Active warning (e.g. storm, avalanche, etc.)
	mCommerce	n.s.	
	Feedback	n.s.	
F-value: 128.18 Sig. of F = .000 Adj. R² = .62			
3. News & Weather	Search & Browse	.363**	Actual news and weather forecasts for various regions
	Recommendation	.189*	Location and preference specific information filter
	Context-aware P.	.484**	Location-, activity- & preference-based actively informs
	mCommerce	n.s.	
	Feedback	n.s.	
F-value: 93.88 Sig. of F = .000 Adj. R² = .54			
4. Event Guide	Search & Browse	.261**	Simple and category-based search
	Recommendation	.313**	Filter for local/regional events during stay period
	Context-aware P.	n.s.	
	mCommerce	n.s.	
	Feedback	.108*	Evaluating and reading customer evaluations
F-value: 49.59 Sig. of F = .001 Adj. R² = .56			
5. Gastronomy & Nightlife	Search & Browse	.435**	Simple and category-based search
	Recommendation	n.s.	
	Context-aware P.	n.s.	
	mCommerce	.181*	Checking occupancies and making reservations
	Feedback	.163*	Evaluating and reading customer evaluations
F-value: 92.21 Sig. of F = .000 Adj. R² = .61			

6. Sightseeing & Shopping	Search & Browse	.373**	Simple and category-based search
	Recommendation	n.s.	
	Context-aware Push	.184*	Act. recommends sights/marts while moving in destination
	mCommerce	.199*	Ticketing (e.g. museums, etc.)
	Feedback	n.s.	
F-value: 42.63 Sig. of F = .001 Adj. R² = 0.51 N=705			
Dependent variable: Intention to Use Sig. of (std.) Beta: ** < 1% * <5% not sig.: n. s.			

Table 1: Use-Intention of Mobile Information Services

Firstly, the employed approach to statistically 'explain' the TAM-variable 'intention to use' a specific information service by its typical functionalities proved to be adequate as for all the six examined mobile services the corresponding regression model showed significant F-values as well as relatively high adjusted R^2 values (i.e., ranging between .41 and .62). Secondly, the search & browse functionality can typically be classified as 'base-functionality' as it proved to be significantly relevant for all the six examined mobile information services. Interesting enough, for a total of four information services the context-aware push functionality seems to play a significant role in determining the 'intention to use' the mobile tourist guide during the destination stay. More precise, for the three most attractive information services in the eyes of the customers, namely (1) transport & navigation, (2) the security assistant and (3) news & weather (Rasinger et al., 2007) the corresponding context-aware push functions are acting as the most prominent functionalities what can be seen from the high and strongly significant (i.e., standardized) regression coefficients (Hair et al., 2005). In addition, push functionalities (significantly) support also the intention to use a mobile information service supporting (6) sightseeing & shopping activities in the destination (see Table 1).

To summarize, in the eyes of the tourists the following information services emerged as highly relevant (corresponding to the push functionality) to improve the acceptance rate for mobile tourist guides (see Table 2):

1.1 Motivation

Information Service	Context based Push Functionality description
Transport & Navigation	In the case of transport-related events (e.g. postponements, congestion, detours, etc.) the system actively informs about delays and proposes alternative routes (e.g. connection flights, busses, etc.).
Security Assistant	While moving within the destination and depending on the individual location the system actively informs about risks (e.g. storm, avalanche, etc.).
News & Weather	Based on location, individual preferences (i.e., areas of interests), and actual (e.g. tourism) activities the system actively informs about the various destination offers and weather conditions/forecasts.
Sightseeing & Shopping	While moving within destination and depending on the location and individual preferences the system actively recommends sights and shopping opportunities

Table 2: Information Services

1.1.2 Example Message Types

This section provides an overview about typical push messages in tourism. The proposed message types are based on the information services which were derived from both the results of the studies concerning usage intention of Rasinger et al. (2007; 2008) and the desired information services posed by prospective service providers. The following five tourism information services were determined:

- general information about the destination
- information related to the destination's weather
- information about events
- information about sights
- information about hotels

Corresponding to these information services four potential message types were specified which are summarized in Table 3. It is worth noting that the same information services may be contained in more than one message type, e.g. event information may be contained within the *Good Morning Message* as well as within the *Event Notification* message type.

message type	message content (information service)	triggering situation
Trip Start	general information	trip start
Good Morning Message	weather, event, and/or sight information	daily
Event Notification	notification about suitable events	x days before the event starts
Hotel	hotel information	on demand

Table 3: Requested Message Types

The *trip start* message type provides subscribed users with general information about the destination to be visited, e.g. security hints or emergency telephone numbers. The information is provided when the trip starts. The *Good Morning* message type informs subscribed users about suitable sights and the current weather of their current destination. This message is provided daily for a selectable time frame. The *Event Notification* message type informs tourists about suitable events which will take place within the next days. This message is sent a few days before the event will take place. The *Hotel* message type provides guests with relevant information regarding their hotel, e.g. that the room entry is possible at 09:00 A.M. instead of 13:00 P.M. Such a message is sent up on request of a service provider.

1.2 Objectives of CAIPS

With the help of a *context-aware information push system* a corresponding service provider may reach his consumers at the *right* time, at the *right* location and provide exactly the *right* information in the *right* situation. Providing a push based channel in addition to traditional pull channels may further improve the communication between supplier and consumer. This is of particular importance in service sectors such as tourism where a strong need for information exchange between the supplier and the consumer side can be observed (Hannes Werthner & Klein, 1999).

From the consumer's point of view CAIPS may optimize his search and planning process by addressing the corresponding key issues, namely *information overload* and *information retrieval effort*. In tourism the consumer's search and planning process is fairly complex and time consuming (Dunstall et al., 2003). Particularly during the on site phase tourists do not have an idea which tourism services to consume or even to look for. CAIPS addresses this problem by providing the user with personalized suggestions informing about tourism services the user might be interested in.

The objectives, classified according to the involved stakeholders, are summarized in Table 4. The stakeholders are discussed in greater detail in Section 3.2.

Stakeholder	Objective
Service Provider	provide tailored information to the consumers
User	reduce search and complexity costs

Table 4: Objectives Classified by Involved Stakeholders

CAIPS was introduced by drawing on scenarios from the tourism industry. However, the approach as proposed in this thesis does not depend on this particular application domain and may be exploited for building context-aware push systems for arbitrary domains.

1.3 Contribution

The fundamental contribution of this thesis is the design of a *conceptual framework* facilitating the design and implementation of context-aware information push systems. Such a system enables the rapid creation of tailored messages without the need to modify the underlying system, i.e., without the trouble of writing new code for new messages. The conceptual framework is composed of a *reference model* and a *rule language framework*. The *reference model* specifies the fundamental functional and logical components aiming to serve as the basis for implementing specific system architectures. The *rule language framework* supports the development of specific rule language instances. The rule language enables the system operator to declaratively create message types and associates them with a situation whose occurrence triggers the creation of tailored and personalized messages.

A further contribution of this thesis is a detailed discussion of basis technologies the design of CAIPS is based on; both their collaboration and their roles within CAIPS are presented.

Moreover, this thesis proposes a novel publish/subscribe approach producing *tailored messages on demand*. This approach stands in contrast to that of traditional publish/subscribe systems. These systems firstly create non-tailored messages and subsequently determine the potential recipients by comparing the messages and the recipient's preferences exploiting different matching techniques.

The design and implementation (based on the conceptual framework mentioned above) of the context-aware information push system "CAIPS-IM" as an integrated part of the mobile tourist information system *innsbruck.mobile* served as a proof of concept.

A case study is provided which discusses the design and implementation of CAIPS-IM. Furthermore, it provides a qualitative evaluation of the conceptual framework.

However, it should be noted that this thesis does not focus on:
- human computer interaction issues such as providing solutions for the interruption of the user when receiving messages
- privacy and security issues
- context modeling
- sensing of contextual data
- business issues

1.4 Thesis Outline

This thesis is structured as follows:

- Section 2 – *Background and Theoretical Foundations*: Expert, context-aware, publish/subscribe and recommender systems are introduced and discussed with respect to the design of the *reference model* proposed in the subsequent section. Additionally, based on principles and concepts of classical knowledge representation theory this section provides the basics for the design of the *Context-Aware Information Triggering Language* (CAITL).

- Section 3 – *Designing CAIPS*: This section is the central part of the thesis. It discusses the fundamental concepts behind the design of CAIPS. First, an overview of CAIPS is provided. Subsequently, the stakeholders of CAIPS are introduced. The functional requirements that are posed by CAIPS and that have to be tackled by an appropriate conceptual framework are also defined here. The main part of this section discusses the conceptual framework facilitating the design and implementation of domain independent, declarative, context-aware information push systems. The conceptual framework is fundamentally composed of a *reference model* (cf. Section 3.5.1) and a *reactive rule language* (cf. Section 3.5.2). Its design was significantly driven by the base systems discussed in Section 2.

- Section 4 – *Case Study: innsbruck.mobile*: This section describes the implementation of CAIPS-IM, a specific CAIPS system drawing on the mobile tourist information system *innsbruck.mobile*. CAIPS-IM was derived from the conceptual framework introduced in Section 3.5. The implementation of CAIPS-IM serves as the proof of concept for the applicability of the proposed framework. Furthermore, based on this implementation a qualitative evaluation is presented, i.e., it is evaluated whether this system meets the requirements as specified in Section 3.3.

- Section 5 – *Related Work*: This section reviews systems related to this thesis and discusses their strengths and shortcomings with respect to CAIPS.

- Section 6 – *Conclusion*: Finally, the conclusion summarizes the contributions of this thesis, critically assesses the shortcomings of the proposed approach, and suggests topics for further research.

2 Background and Theoretical Foundations

> *Those who are enamored of practice without theory are like a pilot*
> *who goes into a ship without rudder or compass and never has*
> *any certainty where he is going*
>
> Leonardo da Vinci (1452 - 1519)

2.1 Knowledge Representation and Expert Systems

This section discusses the fundamentals of *knowledge representation theory* and *expert systems*. The conceptual framework behind CAIPS, which is presented in Section 3.5, is fundamentally influenced by the above mentioned concepts (cf. Section 2.1.4).

Before going into detail the general meaning of *knowledge* is briefly discussed. Literature does not provide a common and unique definition of what knowledge actually means. A survey of different definitions is provided by Zins (2008). Because knowledge representation is a multidisciplinary field comprising computer-science disciplines such as artificial intelligence as well as social science disciplines such as psychology and philosophy the definition varies from discipline to discipline. The meaning of the term knowledge within this thesis agrees with definitions provided by data and knowledge management literature (Bodendorf, 2005; Davenport & Prusak, 2000). Figure 1 illustrates the relationship between *data*, *information*, and *knowledge*:

2.1 Knowledge Representation and Expert Systems

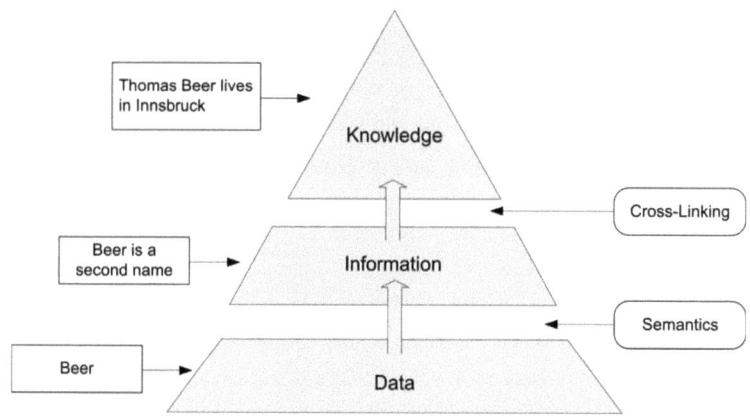

Figure 1: Data - Information - Knowledge

Data is simply a sequence of symbols; *information* is data that has been given a meaning, i.e., semantics. The example in Figure 1 shows that semantics assigns the appropriate meaning to raw data, i.e., the meaning that the symbols *"Beer"* are representing a second name. *Knowledge* is derived by cross-linking information and can be regarded as an individual understanding of information based on its context, i.e., on its relevance to the current domain of discussion.

As discussed in Alavi & Leidner (2005), different types of knowledge can be distinguished. Two famous knowledge types are *declarative* and *procedural* knowledge (Anderson, 1981; Anderson & Lebiere, 1998; Misker & Anderson, 2003). The first refers to representations of objects and how these are interrelated. Other terms found in literature are *descriptive knowledge*, *propositional knowledge*, and *Know-about* which underlines its focus, namely to express knowledge *about* things. Procedural knowledge, also known as *Know-how*, describes knowledge about how to perform and expresses goal specific knowledge.

2.1.1 Knowledge Representation

As intelligent behavior is clearly conditioned by knowledge (Brachman & Levesque, 2004) a powerful mechanism for its representation is required. Davis et al. (1993) argues that the central task of *knowledge representation* (KR) is to capture the complexity of the real world. This task is addressed by the application of multidisciplinary theories and techniques (Sowa, 2000), namely:
- *Ontology*: defines the categories of things that exist in an application domain
- *Logic*: provides inference rules and a formal structure
- *Computation*: implementation in computer programs which distinguishes knowledge representation from pure philosophy

Hence, knowledge representation can be defined as the application of logic and ontology to the task of constructing computable models for some domain. To gain a better understanding of the knowledge representation work of Davis et al. (1993) is exploited; he argues that knowledge representation is best understood in terms of five roles. Each of these roles place different and at times conflicting requirements on the properties of knowledge representations. The roles are introduced and discussed below.

Role I: A KR is a Surrogate

Within the field of artificial intelligence KR provides the base for creating intelligent software entities. All these entities have in common that they try to reason about the real world. However, reasoning is an internal process whereas most things to reason about exist only externally which is known as *inevitable dichotomy*. Inside the reasoner knowledge representations serve as a surrogate for the things existing in the real world. The relations between symbols and things of the real world are analyzed in the famous *meaning triangle* (Ogden & Richards, 1989) which discusses the mapping of a meaning to symbols dependent on the context.

The same goes for operations on representations; these operations are a substitute for direct interaction with the world. Two questions arising with surrogates are how to deal with *identity* and *fidelity*. The first one specifies the correspondence, i.e., the semantics, between the surrogate and its intended representative in the real world. Fidelity deals with the question how close a real thing comes to its appropriate surrogate. It is important to note that perfect fidelity is in general impossible. Certainly, formal objects such as mathematical entities can be exactly captured. Almost any reasoning task has to deal with real world objects as well as formal objects. Therefore, surrogates are pragmatically unavoidable.

Two important consequences arise from this imperfect match. First, it has to be "lied" when representing the real world either through omission or by introducing new artifacts. Second, broad-based reasoning may eventually infer incorrect conclusions independent of both the reasoning process and the representation technology. This can not be avoided by switching to another representation style because all representations are imperfect and therefore a potential source of error. This is the reason why drawing only sound inferences does not free reasoning from errors. It can only ensure that inference is not the source of that error. Choosing an adequate representation is strongly concerned with finding a knowledge representation technology that minimizes this error for the intended application.

Role II: A KR is a Set of Ontological Commitments

As stated above all representations are imperfect and just an approximation to the real world, i.e., there must be a commitment about how the real world is seen. It is impossible to cope with

2.1 Knowledge Representation and Expert Systems

the world in its inherent complexity. *Ontological commitments* define the parts of the world to be focused on at the expense of blurring and/or omitting other parts, i.e., they specify how to see the world. They provide a kind of abstraction of the real world allowing to cope with the otherwise untenable complexity. Ontological commitments are therefore one of the most important contributions a representation may offer. Ontologies can be formulated in various notions and languages such as logic or appropriate ontology languages (see also Section 2.1.2.3). However, the most important thing is the content and not the representation technology, i.e., the set of concepts offered as a way of thinking about the world. Ontological commitments must already be made within the first steps of knowledge representation *(level one)*, i.e., when choosing the appropriate representation technology (cf. Section 2.1.2). All those technologies offer different perspectives of the domain of discourse. Their selection significantly impacts the perception of the world being modeled. Further commitments must be made when the content structure is created, i.e., during identifying appropriate concepts *(level two)*. *Third level* commitments must be made when the structure is populated, i.e., when the identified concepts are instantiated.

Role III: A KR is a Fragmentary Theory of Intelligent Reasoning

Davis et al. (1993) argue that a representation's initial design is usually driven by some insight indicating how people reason intelligently. However, a representation may capture this insight only partial and may only represent a part of the complex process of intelligent reasoning. These are two reasons why the theory is only *fragmentary*. Even if a representation's theory of intelligent reasoning is often only implicit it can be examined in the sense of three components.

The first is the representation's *fundamental conception of intelligent inference* addressing the questions about the meaning of intelligent reasoning in general. This question striving for a definition of intelligent reasoning is often founded on mathematical logic only; this is based on the assumption that intelligent reasoning is a variety of calculation such as deduction in first order logic. However, based on the fields of *psychology*, *biology*, *statistics*, and *economics* Davis et al. (1993) introduced four pretty different views of the nature of intelligent reasoning. The psychological approach, for example, introduces a form of intelligent reasoning which is strongly related to human problem solving behavior which could be viewed in terms of goals, plans, and other complex mental structures. In other words, intelligent reasoning is realized by capturing human expert reasoning.

Several consequences arise from the different positions regarding the nature of intelligent reasoning:

- choosing a knowledge representation technology always means selecting the conception of the fundamental nature of intelligent reasoning as well
- these conceptions differ in important ways leading to different goals, definitions of success, and different artifacts being created

These differences are rarely articulated and may lead to inappropriate system comparisons such as the advantage of sound reasoning in first-order logic compared to the difficulties in characterizing the inferences of frame-based systems. Each one has advantages and disadvantages which may make it the preferred strategy for certain purposes. Sowa (2000) exemplifies this phenomenon through implementing the well known traffic light example in three different representations, namely a procedural loop, a logical formula, and a forward-chaining rule.

The second component, namely the set of inferences the representation *sanctions* addresses the question what can be inferred from what is known. Sanctioned inferences indicate what can be inferred at all. Inferences encompassed by meta-logical implication, i.e., proof rules (Huth & Ryan, 2004) are an example from the field of traditional logic. Besides these inferences which can be made *legally* it is also necessary to indicate the *intelligent* inferences, i.e., the ones which are appropriate to make.

These intelligent inferences are indicated by *recommended* inferences which represent the third component of the theory of intelligent reasoning. They address the question what should be inferred from what is known. Rules in expert systems representing human expertise are an example of recommended inferences.

Role IV: A KR is a Medium for Efficient Computation

From a mechanistic point of view reasoning may be regarded as a pure computational process, or in other words, in order to benefit from a knowledge representation it must be computable. However, this computerized information passes many representation levels shifting the level of abstracting from more physical, real world objects to computer oriented details (Sowa, 2000). In general, two levels, namely the *epistemological* and the *heuristic* level can be distinguished (John McCarthy & Hayes, 1969). The former is concerned with declarative, logic-like knowledge representations about objects and processes of the application domain. The latter introduces data structures for representing theses objects and processes. A more elaborate consideration of these levels was done by Brachman (1979). In his analysis of knowledge representations in semantic networks he introduced five more granular knowledge levels:

2.1 Knowledge Representation and Expert Systems

- *Implementational Level*: This level is similar to the heuristic level introduced above, i.e., the basic data structures are defined on this elementary level
- *Logical Level*: The primitives are propositions, predicates, variables, quantifiers and Boolean operators
- *Epistemological Level*: This level defines concept types, inheritance, and structuring relations
- *Conceptual Level*: This level introduces semantic relations and small sets of language-independent objects
- *Linguistic Level*: The primitives are language-dependent concepts, words, and expressions of natural language

The corresponding "techniques" involved in representing knowledge within *innsbruck.mobile* are (cf. Section 4):

- *Implementational Level*: Hibernate (Hibernate, 2008)
- *Logical Level*: Relational Model
- *Epistemological Level*: Object-Oriented KR
- *Conceptual Level*: Harmonise Ontology (Dell'Erba et al., 2005)
- *Linguistic Level*: Harmonise Ontology

Strongly related to the role as a medium for efficient computation are a language's expressiveness and its computational complexity. The *fundamental tradeoff in knowledge representation* which was introduced by Levesque & Brachman (1985) states that the expressiveness of a knowledge representation language is indirect proportional to its computational tractability, i.e., with increasing expressive power the computational complexity of the reasoning process increases as well.

Representations may provide guidelines for organizing information in ways that support the computability of recommended inferences. For example, the processing of recommended inferences may be facilitated in rule-based representations by exploiting indices leading from facts to conclusions (cf. *forward chaining* in Russel & Norvig, 2003), or from conclusions to facts (cf. *backward chaining* in Russel & Norvig, 2003).

Role V: A KR is a Medium of Human Expression and Communication

A knowledge representation is a medium of communication to tell machines as well as humans about the real world. Since the process of knowledge representation (or knowledge engineering) usually involves experts from various fields such as knowledge engineers and domain experts it is essential that they can communicate in a common, well known language which in turn avoids the jargon of artificial intelligence. One question dealing with this issue is whether a representation can be used as a medium of communication, i.e., how easy is it to communicate using that representation language. It is really a matter of "how easy it is" and not if it would be possible in general or using the words of Davis et al. (1993) "*a representation is the language in which we communicate hence we must be able to speak it without heroic effort*".

2.1.2 Knowledge Representation Technologies

This section briefly introduces the *knowledge representation technologies* CAIPS is based on. Similar to Davis et al. (1993) the term knowledge representation technology denotes individual knowledge representations such as logic or rules. A classification of such technologies is illustrated in Helbig (2001).

2.1.2.1 Object-Oriented Representation Technology

Object-oriented (O-O) concepts are mainly known from two areas, namely software development and artificial intelligence. The former one comprises both object-oriented design and engineering methods (Balzert, 2001; Breu, 2001), and object-oriented programming languages such as Java, C++, or Simula-67 (Dahl et al., 1968).

The latter extensively employed object-oriented concepts for knowledge representation purposes. Inspired by influencing work from Minsky (1975), who emphasized the need for structure in organizing knowledge, *Frames* became popular for representing knowledge. Due to its concurrent development frame-based systems such as NUDGE (Goldstein & Roberts, 1977), or KRL (Bobrow & Winograd, 1977), and object-oriented systems share many of the same intuitions and techniques (Brachman & Levesque, 2004). Frame-based systems, actually representing a family of systems, are based on a common fundamental principle, namely to group both data and procedures by organizing the knowledge within structures. O-O programming systems combine a declarative style to specify objects with a procedural style to define actions upon these objects. The similarity between frame-based and object-oriented systems is obvious. Both have in common that they organize their declarations in a class or type hierarchy which supports the same kind of inference, namely inheritance from *supertypes to subtypes* (e.g. every person has a birth date, a tourist is a person, and therefore every tourist has a birth date). They further support *type- to instance* inheritance (e.g. every person has a birth date, Thomas is a person, and therefore Thomas has a birth date), and *supertype to instance* inheritance (e.g. Thomas is a Tourist, therefore Thomas is a Person).

However, frame-based and O-O systems may be differentiated in the way they allow procedures to access their slots and their instance variables respectively. Frames do not support the well-known O-O *encapsulation* feature which avoids the direct manipulation of private

2.1 Knowledge Representation and Expert Systems

instance variables through external classes or programs (Sowa, 2000). Moreover, frame-based systems usually apply a centralized control component, whereas object-oriented systems tend to be more decentralized having independent objects communicating to each other by sending messages (Brachman & Levesque, 2004).

It is worth to note that the ontology language *F-logic* (Angele & Lausen, 2004), which combines the advantages of frame-based languages and logic, is based on frame theory (cf. Section 2.1.2.3). Furthermore, frames are employed within case-based reasoning systems (cf. Section 2.4) for implementing cases (Jackson, 1999).

2.1.2.2 Rules

Rules are a well studied technique in the field of knowledge representation. They provide an excellent trade-off between understandability and formal requirements. Conditional clauses, i.e., "*if condition, then action*" clauses were already used in pre-Christian times to express activity instructions (Jaynes, 1976). It therefore can be assumed that rules are well known for the user. Using rules addresses one of the prior objectives when designing rule-based expert systems, namely the similarity to human thinking and the consequent improvement of usability (Beierle & Kern-Isberner, 2003). Rules capture guesses of the sort that a human expert makes, guesses that are not necessarily either sound or true in any model (R. Davis et al., 1993). They offer an excellent mechanism for representing both procedural knowledge and recommended inferences (cf. Section 2.1.1).

In literature various rule types are distinguished. Based on work from Berndtsson & Calestam (2003), Berners-Lee et al. (2004), Boley & Tabet (2007), and Eberhart (2002) the subsequent classification of rule types was derived (see Figure 2):

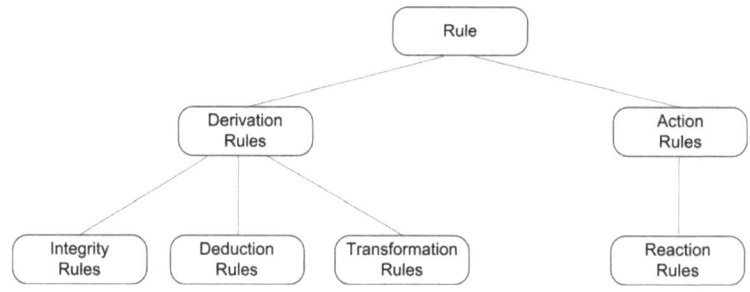

Figure 2: Rule Types

The *reaction* rule type is of special interest for CAIPS because its internal rule language (cf. Section 3.5.2) is based on *Event-Condition-Action* (E-C-A) rules. These rules are well suited for observing state changes and reacting to these changes, i.e., to execute corresponding tasks. Any such a state transition can be regarded as an event. Events may range from real life events such as the arrival of a person in a certain location to system internal events such as the occurrence of a specific point of time published by a timer component[1]. Within CAIPS E-C-A rules are employed for the observation of situations whose occurrences trigger the sending of interdependent information.

As their name implies, E-C-A rules are typical representatives of *reaction* rules (in literature different terms such as *active rules* are synonymously used). E-C-A rules were for the first-time studied in the field of active databases. Related work discussing the usage of E-C-A rules within this research area is provided by Dayal et al. (1994), Elmasri & Navathe (2006), McCarthy & Dayal (1989), Paton & Diaz (1999), and Widom & Ceri (1996). More recently the E-C-A paradigm has gained popularity within the Semantic Web research community for realizing behavior within the semantic web stack (J. Bailey et al., 2005; Bry & Patranjan, 2005; May et al., 2005a; May et al., 2005b; Papamarkos et al., 2003, 2004). Prior to their employment within the Semantic Web stack, E-C-A rules have also been studied in the field of XML repositories (James Bailey et al., 2002; Bonifati et al., 2001).

Except for work from Bry & Patranjan (2005) and May (2005a) all approaches referenced above support only restricted event subscriptions, i.e., they exclusively support subscriptions dealing with update operations in databases, XML stores, or RDF resources (update in terms of covering insert, delete, and update operations). A similar shortcoming can be observed within the action component, i.e., the supported actions are restricted to update operations as well.

Before continuing it should be stated that *conditional clauses* may be considered as a possible approach for implementing specific rule types instead of regarding them as a separate rule type (Hanson & Widom, 1993; Palopoli & Torlone, 1997). Conditional clauses are also known as *production rules* in forward-chaining production systems (Brachman & Levesque, 2004) and *situation-action rules* (Russel & Norvig, 2003). It is tempting to equate conditional clauses with the similar looking logical implication. However, this similarity is rather superficial. Conditional clauses may be regarded as computational advices, whilst a logical implication simply states a kind of axiom, i.e., a truth function which is false when its assumption is true and its conclusion false, and true otherwise.

2.1.2.3 Ontologies

Ontologies have a long history among philosophers, linguists, and knowledge representation researchers (Sowa, 2000; Staab & Studer, 2004). However, the main push for ontologies has

---

[1] The meaning of an *event* is discussed in more detail in Section 2.3.2.1.

occurred with the vision of the *Semantic Web* (Fensel et al., 2003; Berners-Lee et al., 2001). More recently its capabilities for context modeling have been discovered. Several definitions have arisen from its long history and diverse application contexts. However, in computer science the definition of Gruber (1993) has gained wide agreement:

An ontology is a formal explicit specification of a shared conceptualization for a domain of interest.

This definition exposes that the concept of an ontology involves more than a certain implementation or representation technology. It makes clear that an ontology must be specified in a language with formal semantics. This ensures computational interpretability of concepts and relations (Staab & Studer, 2004). The second aspect of this definition is the *social aspect* of creating ontologies. The deriving of involved concepts and their relations must be a community driven process usually involving several stakeholders. Especially in the computer science community the focus is clearly on language aspects such as expressiveness and computability. The second and not less important social aspect is often neglected leading to a strong "technical" perspective when choosing representation technologies. This may lead to inappropriate decisions during application design such as using ontology based data management without the need for its characterizing features such as concept reasoning and semantic consistency checks (not to be confused with consistency in traditional database management systems).

Ontology languages play a particular role within knowledge representation as its design was heavily influenced by several traditional knowledge representation theories and technologies (Staab & Studer, 2004). Ontology languages are embracing numerous concepts known from knowledge representation. For example, F-logic (Angele & Lausen, 2004) is based on both frame-based, and logic-based representation technologies.

2.1.3 Expert Systems

Traditionally, problem-solving knowledge is implicitly tied into a program by the human programmer (Feigenbaum, 1992). *Expert systems,* however, perform their tasks by applying rules of thumb to symbolic structures representing what they believe and reason with (Jackson, 1999; Brachman & Levesque, 2004). They aim to rival the performance of human experts, i.e., to replace human experts in some specific domain of discourse (Feigenbaum, 1992). However, this does not mean that an expert system applies a faithful psychological model of an expert; it rather focuses on an expert's problem solving capabilities concerning a specific, restricted problem domain. In other words, as defined by Jackson (1999), an expert system is a *"computer program that represents and reasons with knowledge of some specialist subject with a view to solving problems or giving advice*". However, even if this definition provides an excellent characterization of an expert system it is in no way an exclusive definition. Literature lacks on a unique and precise definition of an expert system. But, regardless of their definitions all expert systems may be characterized by a number of features they have all in common (Beierle & Kern-Isberner, 2003; Feigenbaum, 1992; Cowell, 1999; Jackson, 1999):

- *simulation of human reasoning*: an expert system simulates an expert's problem solving capabilities, i.e., it simulates human reasoning about a specific domain of discourse instead of simulating the domain itself.
- *reasoning over knowledge representations*: the reasoning is performed over human knowledge which is expressed using specific knowledge representation technologies (cf. Section 2.1.2).
- *strict separation between knowledge and reasoning*: the knowledge representation and the reasoning modules are kept separately; they are referred to as knowledge-base and inference engine. Cowell (1999) used the following equation to underline this separation:

expert system = knowledge-base + inference engine

- *heuristic problem solving*: problems are solved by applying heuristic methods. A heuristic may be compared to a rule of thumb representing a piece of knowledge about how to solve the domain specific problems.
- *explanation of their results*: expert system can explain and trace back their problem solutions and the proposed advices

The DENDRAL program (Lindsay et al., 1980) can be regarded as the progenitor of the class of expert systems (B. G. Buchanan & Duda, 1982; Feigenbaum, 1992). By now expert systems are a mature technology mostly applied in the following typical application scenarios:

- *diagnosis*, e.g. medical diagnosis as realized within the famous MYCIN expert system (B. G. Buchanan & Duda, 1982)
- *configuration*, e.g. configuring computer systems as realized within the XCON expert system (Barker et al., 1989)
- *recommendation*, e.g. knowledge-based recommendation as realized by the Advisor Suite system (Jannach, 2004)

Expert systems may be classified according to the technology they employ for representing their knowledge-base, i.e., how they represent the knowledge of the problem domain and how they reasons with. The most prevalent class of expert systems is that of rule-based systems (Barker et al., 1989; B. G. Buchanan & Duda, 1982; Hayes-Roth, 1985). Further types are, for example, *probabilistic expert systems* (Cowell, 1999), *neural networks* (Gallant, 1993), and

2.1 Knowledge Representation and Expert Systems

case-based reasoning (Ricci & Werthner, 2002; Ricci et al., 2001). For a detailed classification and a survey on expert system developments in the years between 1995 till 2004 it is referred to Liao (2005).

According to work from Beierle & Kern-Isberner (2003), Buchanan & Duda (1982), Feigenbaum (1992), Giarratano & Riley (2004), Jackson (1999), and Nikolopoulos (1997) the architecture of an expert system is mainly composed of six components (see Figure 3):

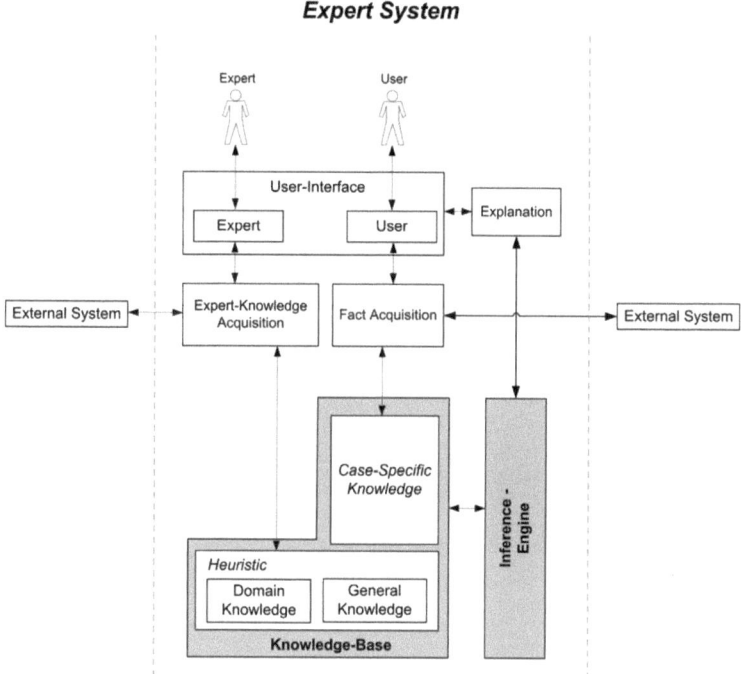

Figure 3: Expert System Overview

- *Knowledge-Base*: Compared to other systems known from AI expert systems store their entire knowledge required for problem solving within a central component, i.e., within the knowledge-base. Its main purpose is to formalize and organize the knowledge to allow the system's reasoning part, i.e., the inference engine, to construct solutions for the associated problem domain. Due to the prevalence of rule-based expert systems it is often suggested that the knowledge-base is exclusively composed of rules. This is misleading because depending on the type of expert system the knowledge-base may also contain probabilistic networks, neural networks, and even no rules at all.

In general the knowledge-base can be separated into two sub-components, namely components storing *case-specific knowledge* and the *heuristics*. The former stores case specific knowledge, i.e., facts for representing the current state of the problem domain. The latter stores both *domain specific* and *general* knowledge, i.e., expert knowledge concerning the problem domain and general knowledge such as general problem solving methods.

- *Inference-Engine*: Embodies the problem solving methodology which is based on the knowledge stored in the knowledge-base.
- *Fact Acquisition*: Maintains the case-specific knowledge which may be acquired from both the user and external systems. It is worth to note that the user and the expert may be the same person.
- *Expert-Knowledge Acquisition*: Maintains the domain and general knowledge which may be acquired from experts as well as from external systems.
- *User-Interface*: Provides interfaces for communicating with the expert system. Usually, separate interfaces are offered for experts and users.
- *Explanation*: Not only the results of an inference process should be presented to the user. An explanation how and why the system came up with specific results may also be provided to the user. This task in realized by the explanation component.

2.1.3.1 Demarcation of Expert Systems

This section briefly discusses approaches similar to expert systems and illustrates their main differences. The motivation for this section was given by the often bewildering way terms such as rule based systems, business rules, deductive databases, and expert systems are used synonymously.

Expert System vs. Rule-Based System

The terms *rule-based* and *expert systems* are often synonymously used. However, rule-based techniques should rather be regarded as one possible approach for building expert systems. Moreover, rule-based systems usually do not operate on knowledge they rather operate on data and are therefore well suited for problem domains with a broad logic.

Literature lacks a unique and precise definition of rule-based systems. Often, the terms rule-based and production systems are used synonymously. Production systems are forward-chaining reasoning systems using production rules (cf. Section 2.1.2.2). It is worth to note that every production system is by definition a rule-based system; however, not every rule-based system in turn is a production system. Similar to expert systems rule-based systems are mainly composed of two *components*, namely a *rule-engine* as well as a *knowledge-base* which in turn consists of the *rule-base* and a *working memory*. Apart from the employment in building expert systems the rule-based approach has gained popularity in the field of rule-based software development aiming to develop highly dynamically applications (Wunderlich, 2006). One mature rule engine easing the development of rule-based systems in Java is Jess (Friedman-Hill, 2003). The application of Jess for building a rule-based system for danger warning in the automotive field is discussed in Beer (2004).

Expert System vs. Business Rules

Primarily, business rules are a mechanism for both explicitly expressing and computationally processing an organization's operational businesses logic, i.e., for describing and implementing the operations and constraints an organization applies to achieve its goals. The business rules approach aims at enhancing the effectiveness, flexibility, and efficiency of business systems. They can be regarded as a key mechanism for engineering the business itself.

According to Jackson's definition of an expert system, a system implementing the business rules paradigm may be regarded as an expert system. This similarity can be underlined by comparing the systems core components. Using the terminology of Ross (2003) a system implementing the business rules mechanism is composed of the following components:

- *Factbase*: The factbase stores the persistent data of the enterprise which are assumed to be accurate and true.
- *Rulebase*: The rulebase stores the declaratively specified business rules.
- *Logicbase*: Is composed of both the fact- and the logicbase.
- *Business logic server*: The runtime system for managing the factbase and executing the rules.

The brief description of each component's tasks reveals the strong relationship between expert and business rules systems. The logicbase and the business logic server may be put on a level with the knowledge-base and the inference engine of an expert system. However, in spite of all these similarities there is one significant difference concerning the key ideas of both mechanisms.

Expert systems aim to provide solutions for specific, restricted problem domains in which they may perform indistinguishable to human experts. The business rules paradigm is not as ambitious; it focuses on organizing and managing the operational business logic and not on other possible forms of knowledge (Ross, 2003; Schacher & Grässle, 2006). Moreover, regarding the implementation of both systems further distinguishing features can be observed.

For example, the rules in rule-based expert systems are usually static[2] compared to those of the business rules paradigm. The latter ensures more agile and flexible business solutions which inherently need to be modified in continuous intervals.

The relationship between database systems and the business rules paradigm is discussed in Date (2000, 2007) and Pascal (Pascal, 2006).

Expert System vs. Relational Databases

In the 1970s experts systems were strongly based on AI programming languages such as Prolog (Colmerauer & Roussel, 1996; Mitchell, 2003). Relational databases, i.e., the underlying relational calculus, and these expert systems have a common logical foundation, namely predicate calculus, or to be more precise, first order logic[3]. This is one reason for the similarity of these early expert systems and today's database management systems (DBMS). However, in spite of these similarities a DBMS should not be regarded as an expert system; its focus is efficient storage and processing of mass data and not to rival the performance of human experts. It should rather be regarded as a technology enhancing the development of expert systems. For a more detailed comparison of database and expert systems it is referred to Bench-Capon (1998).

Expert System vs. Knowledge-Based System

The terms knowledge-based and expert system are sometimes synonymously employed in literature. However, as discussed by Jackson (1999) the former is more general and characterizes a broader collection of systems. For example, a system informing about the current weather may be a knowledge-based system even if it does not apply any expert knowledge in meteorology. However, an expert system in the domain of meteorology is expected to provide forecasts. Both systems have in common that they are usually based on an explicit representation of knowledge and that this knowledge is processed within a self-contained inference engine.

2.1.4 Utilization within CAIPS & Discussion

Due to its importance for this thesis and its influence on following topics such as context-aware and recommender systems the field of knowledge representation was discussed in more detail. Its impacts on the design of CAIPS are briefly summarized subsequently:

---

[2] static in the sense that they are predefined and usually are not modified during runtime

[3] for a detailed discussion contrasting first order logic and relational calculus see Ullmann (1988)

2.2 Context-Aware Systems 27

- KR technologies: Regarding their employment within CAIPS a number of knowledge representation technologies were discussed in more detail:
  - O-O: Employed within CAIPS as a possible context modeling and storing technique (cf. Section 2.2.1). Moreover, their inference capabilities are exploited for the expressive specification of *Message Triggering Situations* (cf. Section 3.4.6). Furthermore, O-O theories established the groundwork for some of today's ontology languages such as F-logic or OWL which in turn can be employed for context-modeling.
  - Rules: They provide the fundamentals to express the heuristic expert knowledge, i.e., to specify *what* should be sent to *whom* and *when*, and to specify the domain expert's knowledge regarding the recommendation of certain items as well.
  - Ontologies: Similar to O-O techniques, ontologies are a well studied context modeling approach (cf. Section 2.2.1) and may be employed within CAIPS for modeling and storing context information.
- Within CAIPS declarative knowledge (i.e., the context-repository, cf. Section 3.5.1.1) and procedural knowledge (i.e., the rules) are strongly intertwined. The declarative knowledge may be regarded as input for the procedural knowledge. Section 2.1.1 has provided the theoretical foundations for an efficient combination of the two knowledge types (cf. Section 3.5.2.1). Hence, it has set the basis for the design of the declarative rule language (cf. Section 3.5.2) which represents the procedural expert knowledge of CAIPS.
- An expert system's architecture significantly inspired the design of the *reference model* (cf. Section 3.5.1). Moreover, the study of expert systems has provided foundation for understanding knowledge-based recommender systems (cf. Section 2.4).

2.2 Context-Aware Systems

This section discusses general concepts regarding the nature of *context* followed by the introduction of architectural principles context-aware systems have in common.

2.2.1 Basics

Numerous applications claiming to be context-aware have been proposed within the last decades. Examples range from tourism information systems[4] such as *Cyberguide* (Abowd et al., 1997), *GUIDE* (Cheverst et al., 2000), *CATIS* (Pashtan et al., 2003), *TIP* (Hinze & Voisard,

---

[4] A detailed survey on context-aware mobile tourism guides is provided by Schwinger et al. (2005).

2003b), or *etPlanner* (Höpken et al., 2006) to ubiquitous computing applications such as the development of smart home environments (Gu et al., 2004a) or the PERSONA project (Hellenschmidt & Wichert, 2007).

The history of context-aware applications started with *The Active Badge Location System* (Want et al., 1992) which already employed a simple form of production rules to perform *context-triggered actions* (Schilit et al., 1994) based on certain location dependent events such as *arriving, departing*, or *settled-in*. The term *context-aware computing* was employed for the first-time by Schilit & Theimer in 1994.

Context-aware systems provide tailored services to the user by incorporating their context; hence, making them more attentive, responsive and aware to the user's environment (Adelstein et al., 2005; Pascoe, 1997; van Kranenburg et al., 2006). Referring to Dey and Abowd (2000b) context-aware systems may be classified into three categories:

- *Automatic execution*: While the first category comprises manually triggered features this category involves the features which are automatically triggered based on the occurrence of a certain contextual state. An example of this category is the automatic sending and creation of personalized messages within CAIPS as described in Section 3. This category is similar to Schilit's *context-triggered actions* and Pascoe's *contextual adaptation*.
- *Tagging of context to information to support later retrieval*: This feature describes applications which augment the environment with extra information by associating a *particular* context with additional information. This category is similar to Pascoe's *contextual augmentation*. An example of this category is the InfoArea project (Vogt et al., 2007; Sengaro GmbH, 2009) allowing the tagging of arbitrary information with location specific data. The tagged information is automatically presented on the user's mobile when he approaches a respective location, i.e., a location which was previously assigned to a specific information. Therfore, the InfoArea project can also be regarded as an example of the automatic execution category.
- *Presentation*: This category comprises all features aiming at presenting contextual information or services to the user. This category is a combination of *proximate selection* and *contextual commands* as discussed in Schilit et al. (1994). Examples of this category are the emphasizing of objects that are located nearby or the sending of print commands to the nearest printer. CAIPS as well as the InfoArea project mentioned above are further representatives of this system category.

The first applications claiming being context-aware were primarily focused on location as the only characterizing criteria of an entity's context; however, it is important to note that context comprises much more than just location. Therefore, when designing context-aware systems it is

2.2 Context-Aware Systems

inalienable to have a solid understanding of *context* as it supports to choose the appropriate contextual information and to determine the application's desired context-aware behavior (Dey, 2001). Attempts to find elaborate definitions of context have been proposed by numerous researchers such as Dey & Abowd (2000b), Chen & Kotz (2000), Henricksen (2003), Pascoe (1998), Ryan et al. (1997), Schilit & Theimer (1994), or Schmidt et al., 1999. Most of the proposed definitions fall into two broad categories, namely enumeration- and role-based. The first tries to define context by enumerating examples or categories. The second defines context in terms of its role in context-aware computing (Adelstein et al., 2005). As it changes from application to application it is not possible to provide a solid definition by enumerating contextual categories; for example, temporal aspects such as the current time may be exploited by one application, whereas a second application does not require incorporating temporal aspects. In the first case, the current time affects the applications behavior and therefore it is regarded as context. However, in the second case, the current time does not affect the behavior and therefore it is not considered as context.

Within this thesis the meaning of context agrees with Dey & Abowd's (2000b) operational definition:

Context is any information that can be used to characterize the situation of an entity. An entity is a person, a place, or object that is considered relevant to the interaction between a user and an application, including the user and applications themselves.

However, based on work from Chen & Kotz (2000) a possible categorization of context is discussed briefly to get a more powerful understanding of the nature of context. They propose the following context categories:

- *Computing*: Typical instances of this category are the available bandwidth, a display's current resolution, or the device type
- *User*: Typical instances of this category are the user's master data such as age, gender, or his current location
- *Physical*: Typical instances of this category are the current weather, or current traffic conditions
- *Time*: Typical instances of this category are the current time of day, or the season of the year
- *Context History*: This category embraces recordings of the other categories across a certain time period

After having introduced these fundamentals regarding the nature of context context-aware systems can be now defined as follows, exploiting a definition of Dey and Abowd (2000b) as well:

A system is context-aware if it uses context to provide relevant information and/or services to the user, where relevancy depends on the user's task.

Developing context-aware systems is a complex task which is inherently caused by the nature of contextual information (Adelstein et al., 2005). Some of the characteristics of contextual information considered from the perspective of system design are enumerated below:

- In general, context information may be of *physical* or *logical* nature[5] (Hofer et al., 2003). The former represents measurable context information such as acquired by location and temperature hardware sensors. The latter represents more abstract information such as the user-system interaction history, or a user's personal calendar. Context information is provided by several sources, hence acquiring these information is a highly heterogeneous and distributed task.
- It may be necessary to acquire the same type of contextual information from different sources at different times such as GPS is employed for outside location detection and RFID technology for indoor location detection.
- Several abstraction levels may be required to provide contextual information in a form employable by higher level applications. For example, the latitude and longitude data of GPS coordinate are transformed into user appropriate location information such as user has reached the "Golden Roof" in Innsbruck.
- In highly dynamic environments such as mobile applications context changes are required to be detected and reported in real time to support, for example, proactive behavior triggered by context changes.
- Context information may be imperfect, for example, if multiple context sources provide different information regarding the same context instance.

Regardless of its sophisticated nature a well designed context model is a prerequisite for a sound context-aware application as it defines and stores context information in a machine processable form. As mentioned above, numerous context-aware applications have been developed over the years. They range from applications incorporating the physical context only

---

[5] A further classification is provided by Henricksen and Indulska (2004) which distinguishes sensed, static, profiled, and derived context information.

2.2 Context-Aware Systems

(such as adapting the display resolution of mobile devices) to highly complex ubiquitous applications incorporating context information of several context categories. This led to several modeling approaches addressing the different requirements of context-aware applications. Subsequently, common modeling techniques are briefly discussed, namely *graphical, object-oriented*, and *ontology based* models:

- *Graphical Models*: Graphical context models are mainly employed for describing contextual knowledge conceptually. This approach may be compared to the *conceptual* information level introduced in the *four-schema architecture* of information systems (Date, 2004; van Griethuysen, 1982; Elmasri & Navathe, 2006; Halpin, 2001). Typical representatives of graphical modeling techniques are the *Unifified Modeling Language* (UML), the *Entity Relationship Model* (ER), and *Object Role Modeling* (ORM). An example for modeling context using the general purpose language UML is provided by work from Sheng & Benatallah (2005), modeling context using ORM and its mapping to ER is discussed in Henricksen (2003). The computational support for processing graphical models is relatively low as their focus lies primarily on clear communication and information representation in a basic and human understandable way.

- *Object-Oriented models*: Object-oriented knowledge representation was already discussed in detail in Section 2.1.2.1. As stated in that section, the main benefits of O-O approaches are encapsulation, inheritance, and reusability. These features are key enablers for representing the specific characteristics inherent to context information. Examples of object-oriented context models are provided by Belotti et al. (2005) and Hofer et al. (2003).

- *Ontology based modeling*: Recently, ontology based context models have become more popular. Examples of these models within context-aware applications are discussed in Chen et al. (2003) and Gu et al. (2004c). Both approaches employ the *Ontology Web Language* (OWL) (Antoniou & van Harmelen, 2004; Lacy, 2005; McGuinness & van Harmelen, 2004) for representing context.

A detailed discussion including an evaluation of the appropriateness of several modeling approaches for ubiquitous computing is provided by Strang & Linnhoff-Popien (2004). Their evaluation illustrated that O-O and ontology based context models fulfill most of the requirements posed by ubiquitous computing systems. The evaluation was based on six requirements, namely *distributed composition, partial validation, richness and quality of information, incompleteness and ambiguity, level of formality*, and *applicability to existing environments*.

2.2.2 Architecture

The development of context-aware applications follows a common architectural style comprising the following components providing the fundamental services of each context-aware system (Gu et al., 2004b ;van Kranenburg et al., 2006):

- *gathering* contextual data
- *processing & managing* contextual data
- *distributing* contextual data

Based on work[6] of Adelstein et al. (2005), Baldauf et al. (2007), Henricksen (2003), Henricksen et al. (2005), Gu et al. (2004a; 2004b), Hofer et al. (2003), van Kranenburg et al. (2006), and Singh & Conway (2006) the architectural schema, i.e., the layered design as well as the fundamental components context-aware systems have in common is discussed subsequently. The proposed approaches mainly differ in the granularity of the proposed layers; while some propose a three layered schema (Hofer et al., 2003) others apply up to six layers (Henricksen, 2003).

- *Context retrieval layer*: This layer is responsible for gathering raw context information. It usually comprises a set of sensors and their appropriate interaction interfaces. Indulska and Sutton (2003) distinguishes three types of sensors, namely *physical* such as GPS or RFID, *virtual* such as determining a user's location using his calendar, and *logical* sensors such as detecting a user's current location exploiting his last login at his office PC. The interaction interfaces such as low level driver or high-level application programming interfaces are often encapsulated within reusable components; an example of such a component is the *context provider* component as proposed by Gu et al. (2004a). According to the two involved entities this layer is sometimes further separated into two sub layers such as a *raw data retrieval* and a *sensor layer* as proposed in Baldauf et al. (2007).

- *Context preprocessing layer*: This layer is responsible for providing high-level contexts by *aggregating*, *reasoning*, and *interpreting* over low-level contexts. Aggregation and reasoning deals with the combination of context atoms to high-level contexts such as determining whether a user is sleeping by analyzing various physical sensors such as location and light sensors (Gu et al., 2004a). High-level contexts are further formed by interpreting low level context data such as determining a user's location by mapping his RFID chip to his personal id as implemented in the *intelligent location based information*

---

[6] some of these projects are discussed in more detail in section 5

2.2 Context-Aware Systems

(*ilbi*) project (ilbi, 2008). Moreover, components providing conflict resolution functionalities are part of the preprocessing layer as well; an example is to determine the right information source if the same contextual information is provided by different context sources.

- *Context management and storage layer*: This layer is responsible for maintaining the context information gathered at the underneath layers. One of its fundamental components is the *context repository* acting as a common pool for storing context information[7]. It stores both current and historical context information. Obviously, its representation is heavily influenced by the employed context modeling approach. The repository is complemented with an access service providing both synchronous query and asynchronous subscription functionalities.

  Further components residing in this layer are *service discovery* and *management* components. The former offers registry functionality for locating desired services. The latter provides typical management services such as the controlling of user policies.

- *Application layer*: The application logic employing the context information acquired in the aforementioned layers is encapsulated within this layer.

  In short, this layer encapsulates the *application logic*, the three aforementioned layers encapsulate the *middleware* providing fundamental services most context-aware applications have in common. Several frameworks have been developed aiming to facilitate the development of context-aware applications; examples are provided by Hofer et al. (2003), Schwinger et al. (2006), van Kranenburg et al. (2006), and Henricksen et al. (2005).

However, only a few of these approaches such as the *SOCAM* project (Gu et al., 2004c), provide infrastructural support such as partially implemented components or services in addition to their conceptual support.

The layers, their responsibilities as well as an associated example from CAIPS are summarized in Table 5:

---

[7] Comparing to *description logics* (Baader et al., 2004) the repository comprises *terminological* (T- Box) as well as *assertional* knowledge (A-Box)

Layer	Responsibility	CAIPS
application	application logic	rule-based message sending
context management/storage	storage of high-level context information	CAIPS context repository
context preprocessing	aggregation, abstraction, interpretation, conflict resolution	e.g. temperature interpretation
context retrieval	aquisition of sensed data	ZAMG weather web-service

Table 5: Layers of a Context-Aware System

2.2.3 Utilization within CAIPS & Discussion

Considered from a software architectural perspective the central idea behind the design of CAIPS is the synthesis of a set of well-known system types, i.e., to combine *expert systems* with *event-notification*, *context-aware*, and *recommender* systems (cf. Section 3.5.1). CAIPS is heavily based on context-aware and expert systems. Hence, these two types of systems act as a kind of framework for embedding the remaining components. The design of CAIPS was strongly influenced by principles and ideas originating from the field of these two systems.

A solid understanding of the sophisticated nature of context information as well as of context modeling approaches provides the fundamentals for an efficient and sound combination of knowledge-based and context-aware techniques regarding both system design (cf. Section 3.5.1) and the development of the novel *Context-Aware Information Triggering Language* (cf. Section 3.5.2).

2.3 Publish/Subscribe Systems

This section discusses the fundamentals of publish/subscribe systems and their usage within CAIPS. In literature different terms are used for publish/subscribe systems; the most important ones are discussed briefly in Section 2.3.1. The fundamental components of publish/subscribe systems are introduced in Section 2.3.2. In literature the term publish/subscribe (PS) is used for both a kind of *interaction style* and a *type of event-based system*. Section 2.3.3 introduces a taxonomy of interaction models and discusses the publish/subscribe style in more detail. The essence of subscription languages and its significance for CAIPS are discussed in Section 2.3.4. Finally, the relationship between CAIPS and publish/subscribe systems, i.e., how publish/subscribe is exploited within CAIPS is discussed in Section 2.3.5.

2.3.1 Terminology of Publish/Subscribe Systems

Unfortunately, as exposed by Hinze (2003) research literature lacks on a precise definition for publish/subscribe systems. In addition to a missing precise definition different terms are used synonymously for publish/subscribe systems. The most important ones are briefly discussed below.

Event Notification Service

The term *event notification service* (abbreviated: *notification service* or *event service*) is sometimes used synonymously for publish/subscribe systems (Hinze, 2003). Within this thesis this term stands for the mediating component of publish/subscribe systems (cf. Section 2.3.2).

Event-Based Systems

As implied by its denomination *event-based systems* heavily employ the event-based publish/subscribe interaction style (cf. Section 2.3.3). The term event-based system is often used synonymously to publish/subscribe systems (Mühl et al., 2006). This thesis agrees with the point of view of Mühl et al. (2006) and does not distinguish between event-based and publish/subscribe systems.

Alerting Service

Alerting services were originally exploited for warning their users in case of a hazard, intrusion, or engine failure (Hinze, 2003). Today this term is widespread in the field of digital libraries such as Springer Link Alert (Springer, 2008), Elsevier Table of Content (Elsevier, 2005), or IEEE Xplore alert (IEEE Xplore, 2008). For more details about alerting services it is referred to Buchanan et al. (2005).

Services for Selective Dissemination of Information

Systems for "selective dissemination of information" were introduced in the 60's and these systems are similar to event-based systems. For more details it is referred to Altinel & Franklin (2000), Housman & Kaskela (1970), Salton (1968), and Yan & Garcia-Molina (1994).

Reminder Services

Reminder services are exploited to remind their users about important happenings. Example applications and more details are discussed in Beigl (2000) and Marmasse & Schmandt (2000).

2.3.2 Structure

Based on work from Hinze (2003), Mühl (2002), Mühl et al. (2006), and Zeidler (2004) this section discusses the fundamental components of *event-based publish/subscribe systems*. Typical application scenarios range from information dissemination, network monitoring, enterprise application integration, up to mobile and ubiquitous systems (Mühl et al., 2006). As mentioned above, literature lacks a common, unambiguous definition of publish/subscribe systems. Therefore, this section discusses the fundamental items of a publish/subscribe system as employed within this thesis.

The fundamental design of such a system is sketched in Figure 4:

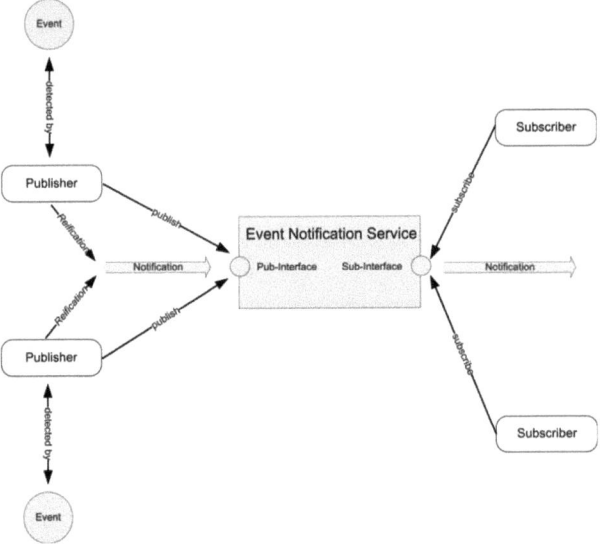

Figure 4: Publish/Subscribe System

A publish/subscribe system is usually composed of the following entities: *Events* and *notifications* as means of state transitions and communication respectively, *producers* and *consumers* as interacting components, *subscriptions* as an indication of interest in certain notifications and the *event notification service* to connect the interacting components. These entities are explained subsequently.

2.3.2.1 Events and Notifications

As its name implies an *event* plays a central role within event-based systems. Items provided by producers such as news, persons detected by sensors, or stocks are represented via *information objects* (Hinze, 2003). Information objects may represent persistent (e.g. documents)

2.3 Publish/Subscribe Systems

or transient (e.g. measured system values) items. Any state transition of an *information object* may be regarded as an event. Events range from observations in the physical world (e.g. detected persons) to arbitrary detection of happenings inside a computer system (e.g. a timer event, or database changes). Further, as identified by Luckham (2002) triggering may occur by a wide scope of events ranging form low-level hardware interrupts up to business-level events. Similar to Hinze & Voisard (2003a) CAIPS distinguishes *internal* and *external* events (cf. Section 3.5.1.5). A more elaborated discussion concerning events is presented in Hinze (2003).

A *notification* contains data describing the observed happening (i.e., the event), often called reification (Zeidler, 2004). The observer of an event is responsible for creating notifications. In addition to the pure indication of a occurrence notifications may store information about the circumstances of the event such as the time of occurrence. An example of the provision of such meta information is given in Bacon et al. (1996). It is worth noting that different notifications can represent the same event, however, from different perspectives. Appropriate data models for representing notifications are name/value pairs, objects, and semi-structured data such as XML. At lower system levels notifications are delivered as materialized *messages* to the event notification service.

2.3.2.2 Producers and Consumers

The interacting components of event-based systems are *producer* and *consumer* software components. In literature they are also known as *publisher and subscriber*, or *provider and client* components (Bazinette et al., 2001; Fiege et al., 2003a; Hinze, 2003; Lehner & Hümmer, 2001). Producers (or publishers) are self-contained components which are responsible for observing its own state and for reporting (i.e., to publish) happenings of interest (i.e., notifications). Self-contained in this sense means that the published notification depends on the producer's internal computation only. Instead of sending published notifications directly to interested consumers they are delivered to the mediating *event notification service* (cf. Section 2.3.2.4). Publishers do not have to know their subscribers. Also, they are unaware of any other components involved and do not expect a response from the consumer side. This loosely coupled approach is also known as *decoupling in space* (Eugster et al., 2003).

Consumers (also known as subscribers) are the counterpart on the other side of the communication path. They state their interest in certain notifications by issuing subscriptions. Subscriptions are discussed in more detail below. Similar to the producer component consumers are unaware of other involved components.

Finally, it is worth noting that these components may act both as producers as well as consumers, i.e., their roles are not strictly separated.

2.3.2.3 Subscriptions

As mentioned above, a subscriber specifies his interests regarding notifications by issuing subscriptions. Hinze (2003) introduces an equivalent concept, namely profiles (query and parameter profiles) to describe a consumer's interest in particular notifications.

To issue a subscription the subscriber submits his interests to the event notification service which in turn is responsible for the evaluation of the subscriptions. Subscriptions may be compared to filters whose intended function is to exclude undesired information and to exactly specify one's information demand. In addition to Boolean valued functions (Mühl et al., 2006) filters may comprise metadata such as timing information to get past notifications (Cilia et al., 2003). From a software engineering viewpoint subscriptions may be regarded as *input interfaces* of consumers.

The complementing items at the producer side are *advertisements* specifying the structure of the notifications they will provide. Furthermore, advertisements are exploited to improve routing decisions in distributed event notifications services (Zeidler, 2004). From a software engineering viewpoint advertisements can be regarded as *output interfaces*.

One crucial aspect influencing the flexibility of event-based systems is the expressiveness of subscriptions regarding its filtering capabilities. Expressiveness and scalability are interdependent and are heavily influenced by the notification selection mechanism, i.e., by the underlying filter models. Therefore, this mechanism must be carefully selected. The most prominent filter models, namely *channels*, *subjects*, *types*, and *content-based*, are briefly discussed below.

Channels

Channels are one of the earliest subscription paradigms. The mapping of published notifications to the interested subscribers is realized via channels. The publisher sends notifications to certain named channels and subscribers in turn specify their interests by choosing a channel. So, the subscribers receive all notifications published to this channel. An example of this notification selection mechanism is the CORBA Notification Service (OMG, 2004).

Subjects

Within the *subject-based* filtering model the subjects (also denoted as topics) are arranged in hierarchies and denoted with path-like character strings (similar to file systems). Publishers annotate each notification with a character string denoting a rooted path in the tree of available subjects. Notification selection is realized using pattern matching (Zeidler, 2004). Subject-based subscriptions are exemplified in Figure 5:

2.3 Publish/Subscribe Systems

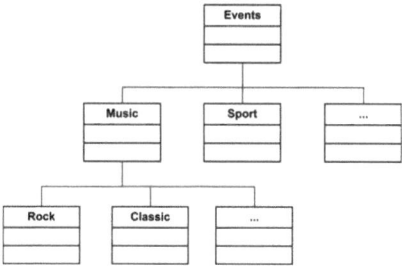

Figure 5: subject-based subscription

Events/Music/Rock represents, for example, a subject string which may occur within a destination information system. Information producers annotate all *rock music events* with this subject string and all subscribers subscribing to *Events/Music/Rock* will get information about rock events.

Content-Based

Content-based notification selection introduces a subscription mechanism based on the actual content of notifications. Notifications are not filtered according to predefined categories but according to the properties of the notifications itself. These properties can be represented by attributes of the employed data model as well as by metadata enriched notifications.

Subscribers specify their interests by issuing subscriptions, i.e., by defining filter restrictions exactly specifying their information demand. Available solutions range from *filter languages* and *template matching* to elaborate *subscription languages* (Bacon et al., 2000; Hinze, 2003; Mühl et al., 2006). The former usually expresses the filter constraints in the form of attribute-value pairs and comparison operators such as "=, <, >, <=, >=, !=". The latter supports the specification of complex filters such as the correlation of events. For details concerning subscription languages it is referred to Section 2.3.4.

Types

Type-based filtering extends subject-based filtering with *types*. Contrasted to subject-based filtering the type-based approach supports multiple inheritance allowing different rooted paths to the same subject, i.e., a subject may have several super-subjects (Eugster et al., 2003; Zeidler, 2004). A subscription to a type means that the subscriber will receive all objects of this type and of all of its subtypes. In general this approach may be considered as a high-level variant of publish/subscribe systems aiming to facilitate the development of subject- and content-based filter approaches ensuring type safety and encapsulation (Eugster, 2007).

2.3.2.4 Event Notification Service

The fundamental component of each event-based system is the *event notification service*. Such a service offers functionalities for the mediation between producers and consumers, i.e., it offers services for storage, management, and efficient delivery of notifications. It tests notifications (received from producers) for matching subscriptions (got from consumers) and forwards successfully matched notifications to the appropriate consumers. From a software engineering viewpoint such a service implements the *publish/subscribe interfaces* offering advertise, publish, subscribe, unsubscribe, and notify methods. The notification service decouples the interacting components by evaluating the subscriptions on behalf of the consumers and by forwarding notifications on behalf of the producers. From the viewpoint of other involved components the event notification service is a black-box (Mühl et al., 2006). According to Eugster et al. (2003) the decoupling of publish/subscribe systems is divided into three dimensions:

Space

The interacting components do not need to know each other

Time

The interacting components do not have to participate at the same time

Synchronization

Producers are not blocked while creating notifications, consumers are not blocked while receiving notifications

2.3.3 Models of Interaction & Abstraction Levels

Mühl et al. (2006) argue that event-based interaction is mainly characterized by the involved components and not by the underlying communication style. Fiege et al. (2003b) and Mühl et al. (2006) distinguish four interaction models illustrating how the interdependencies between the components are established (cf. Table 6):

		Initiator	
		Consumer	*Producer*
Addressee	*Direct*	Request/Reply	Callback
	Indirect	Anonymous Request/Reply	Event-Based Publish/Subscribe

Table 6: Interaction Models

2.3 Publish/Subscribe Systems

The four models are characterized by two attributes, namely *initiator* and *addressee*. The initiator specifies who has started the interaction; the addressee specifies whether the recipient is known or unknown, i.e., whether the peer component is directly or indirectly addressed. It must be noted that the interaction models must not be confused with employed implementation technologies. In general, each interaction model can be implemented by several implementation techniques. An event-based service employing only a few interacting entities may, for example, be realized by using a request/reply based remote procedure call (Birrell & Nelson, 1984; Marshall, 1999; Sun Microsystems Inc., 2008b; UserLand Software, 2003). The interaction model must be carefully chosen because it strongly influences the design of a system. The combination of the two basic attributes leads to four interaction models which support system architects in identifying the basic structure of the components involved. By its clear separation of *computation* from *communication* it moreover supports to avoid confusing interaction and implementation issues. Based on work from Fiege et al. (2003b) and Mühl et al. (2006) the four cooperation models are discussed shortly below:

Request/Reply

The request/reply interaction paradigm is an interaction model which is frequently applied. Prominent examples are any kind of remote procedure call (RPC) or method calls in common. The consumer initiates the interaction by requesting data from the provider. The consumer directly addresses the known producer and expects a reply from him. The incorporation of information about the producer's state into his own state leads to a tight coupling of the interacting components.

Anonymous Request/Reply

As implied by its name this interaction paradigm is also based on the request/reply interaction model. However, compared to the standard request/reply communication model the provider who is responsible for processing the request is not specified. The requests are sent to an arbitrary, possibly dynamically determined set of recipients. This interaction model is often confused with event-based models because anonymous request/reply is directly implemented by publish/subscribe systems (Oki et al., 1993). Even when anonymity of the providers makes the request/reply model more flexible the tight coupling of the interacting components is still omnipresent. Examples of this interaction model are load balancing services selecting the adequate provider at runtime based on the content of the request, or lightweight containers employing the *Dependency Injection Pattern* (Apache Software Foundation, 2007; Fowler, 2004; Spring Source, 2006).

Callback

The well known *observer* design pattern (Gamma et al., 1995; Meyer, 1997) employs the *callback* interaction model. The consumers state their interests in a certain event by posing a condition to a specific, known provider. The provider is responsible for calling back the interested consumers and obviously, for evaluating the condition. The identity of the involved components must be managed on both sides which in turns lead to a tight coupling (no mediator medium is employed).

Event-Based Publish/Subscribe

The characteristics of the *Event-Based* interaction model are inverse to those of the request/reply paradigm, i.e., the communication is initiated by the provider. The notifications are not sent to a specific set of recipients. Compared to the callback model, providers are not responsible for subscription management, i.e., to interpret and administer the subscriptions. As already stated above, components of event-based systems are self-contained, i.e., the encoded knowledge is limited to the component's own task. This characteristic supports the strict separation of the internals of the components of an event-based system. The orchestration of these components is realized within an *external* component and not longer by the components itself.

Compared to the request/reply interaction model the event-based model is marked by flexibility, whereas the former is marked by its simplicity, i.e., it is easy to implement, handle, and understand. Despite the dichotomy of these models they form a duality in the sense that most applications can be realized based on either model. Scalability must be carefully traded off against flexibility on the one hand, and simplicity on the other hand, i.e., system architects have to choose between a simple implementation and an extensible solution.

The event-based publish/subscribe communication paradigm is employed at different system levels of abstraction. Hinze (2003) distinguishes four levels of abstraction, each increasing the grade of abstraction:

- Application Level
- Middleware Level
- Implementation Level
- Operating System

It is important to note that the employment of the event-based interaction style does not necessarily require the event-based model at the next lower abstraction level.

2.3 Publish/Subscribe Systems

Application dependent client profiles (cf. subscription in Section 2.3.2.3) affect the system as a whole and are handled at the *application* level. External sources are filtered and observed by the application. Example services can be found in Carzaniga (1998), Carzaniga et al. (2001), Liu & Jacobsen (2004), Pereira et al. (2001), Ramakrishnan & Dayal (1998), Strom et al. (1998), and Yan & Molina (1995).

Distributed software components communicate using the *middleware* level by encapsulating and transporting events from the higher application level. The inner structure and its interpretation are unknown at this level. Rather, events are regarded as pure data to be processed. Examples for middleware event-based services are discussed in IBM TJ Watson Reseach Center (2001), OMG (2004), Pietzuch (2004), and Sun Microsystems Inc. (2002).

Internal events (cf. Section 2.3.2.1) are detected and reported at the *implementation* level; an example is a trigger in active database systems (Paton & Díaz, 1999). A further example for the application of the event-based style at the implementation level is given by Gawlick & Mishra (2003). For details concerning event detection and detection strategies it is referred to Gehani et al. (1993), Hinze (2003), Li et al. (2004), and Pietzuch et al. (2004).

Synchronization of system tasks and transaction monitors are typical representatives of events at the *operating system* level. Low-level event handling in programming languages or in GUI frameworks such as Java Swing (Sun Microsystems Inc., 2008a), or SWT (Eclipse Foundation, 2008b) are handled at this level.

An elaborate overview of existing standards, commercial systems, and research prototypes is presented in Mühl et al. (2006).

2.3.4 Subscription Language & Event Algebra

Elaborate subscription languages such as those applied within *A-MEDIAS* (Hinze, 2003) and *Siena* (Carzaniga et al., 2000) are usually based on *event algebras* which enable the system to react to sophisticated occurrences of events using an algebra (Carlson & Lisper, 2003). These sophisticated situations may be represented through *composite events* (Hinze, 2003; Mühl et al., 2006) which are composed of *primitive events;* primitive events are also known as *atomic events* (May et al., 2005b). Composite events provide a higher-level abstraction for subscribing to a set of primitive events, therefore, preventing subscribers to handle a large number of primitive events. Hence, subscribers can directly subscribe to sophisticated event occurrences instead of having to subscribe to each primitive event separately and having to perform the detection themselves (Mühl et al., 2006). One advantage of this mechanism is the clear separation of the possibly complex and resource intensive event detection and the system's business logic.

Event algebras support the specification of composite events by defining statements built by the nested application of appropriate operators (such as disjunction, conjunction, negation, or sequence) over primitive events. The semantics of an operator specifies the meaning of a composite event. The detection of a composite event specifies the final state of its contributing sub-events. Several event algebras have been defined for different application domains such as active database systems (Chakravarthy et al., 1994; Chakravarthy & Mishra, 1994; Gehani et al., 1993) or event notification services (Hinze, 2003). Carlson & Lisper (2003) proposed an event algebra supporting restriction policies which are focused on the specific constraints of mobile systems. Moreover, event algebras may be exploited for evaluating the complexity of different services, to check subscriptions for inconsistencies, and as a solid and exactly defined specification for implementing event-filter algorithms (Hinze, 2003).

Situation and event calculus (J. McCarthy, 1989; John McCarthy & Hayes, 1969; Russel & Norvig, 2003; Shanahan, 1999) are similar techniques from the field of knowledge representation. They are popular logic-based methods for reasoning about change, i.e., of using first-order logic to reason about actions and their resulting situations. However, they are focused on reasoning about the occurrence of certain events, whereas event algebras are focused on the detection of complex events.

Based on work from Hinze (2003) the most popular operators for building composite events are discussed subsequently. Hinze distinguishes *event instances* (denoted by a lower case e) and *event classes* (denoted by an upper case E). The former refer to the actual occurrence of an event while the latter are created by event queries such as all users crossing a certain location.

- *Temporal Disjunction*: Composite events formed by the *temporal disjunction operator* $(E_1 \mid E_2)$ occur if either e_1 or e_2 occurs.
- *Temporal Conjunction*: Composite events formed by the temporal *conjunction operator* $(E_1, E_2)_T$ occur if both e_1 and e_2 occur within a certain interval which is defined by a temporal parameter T.
- *Temporal Sequence*: Composite events formed by the *temporal sequence operator* $(E_1; E_2)_T$ occur when first e_1 and afterwards e_2 occurs. Similar to the temporal conjunction operator the temporal distance of the events is defined by a temporal parameter T.
- *Temporal Negation*: The *temporal negation operator* $\bar{E}_T$ forms a passive event, i.e., it occurs if no event instance of the event class E occurs within a certain interval which is defined by the temporal parameter T.
- *Temporal Selection*: Composite events formed by the *temporal selection operator* $E^{[i]}$ occur if the ith event of a sequence of events of the event class E occurs.

In contrast to other event algebras the event algebra proposed by Hinze (2003) can be parameterized thereby enabling an application or use case dependent semantics of the temporal event operators introduced above. Among other things, the parameterized algebra supports to specify how *duplicate instances*[8] should be handled; for example, the algebra supports to specify whether all duplicates or only the first occurrence should be considered. This use case is of special interest for event detection in the field of context-aware information push systems concerning the avoidance of *Duplicate Messages* (cf. Section 3.4.7).

Providing parametrizable operators increases the expressiveness of the algebra regarding filter capabilities and thus the expressiveness of the subscription languages based on this algebra as well.

2.3.5 Utilization within CAIPS & Discussion

The publish/subscribe paradigm is employed within CAIPS in two different ways:
- From a user's perspective CAIPS may be considered as a publish/subscribe system. It provides *Message Types* (cf. Section 3.4.1) the user may subscribe for. These *Message Types* could be compared to channels in content-based subscriptions (cf. Section 2.3.2.3).
- As a key enabler for the rule-based control of the entire messaging process (cf. Section 3.1): The notification selection mechanism heavily influences the expressiveness of the selection of potential message receivers (cf. *Message Triggering Situation* in Section 3.5.2); therefore, supporting complex filter definitions exploiting subscription languages significantly raises the expressiveness of the specification of a *Message Triggering Situation*.

Moreover, the event-based architectural style is heavily applied within CAIPS. One important characteristic all publish/subscribe systems have in common is that publishers and subscribers are not connected directly, i.e., neither the published notifications nor the subscriptions are directed towards specific components. This is also known as the *power of an event-based architectural style* (Carzaniga et al., 1998). Event-based systems have a clear separation between computation and communication, hence supporting the development of easily extendable systems. As already discussed in Section 2.2, context-aware systems are inherently based on the distributed architectural style. Among other things, an infrastructure for such systems has to cope with reconfigurations making this architectural style pertinent for these kind of applications (Cugola & Jacobsen, 2002; Fiege et al., 2003a; Mühl et al., 2006). Event-based architectures

---

[8] *duplicate instances* are all event instances formed by the same event query

support the easy integration of autonomous, heterogeneous components into distributed, complex systems (Bates et al., 1998; Mühl et al., 2006; Sullivan & Notkin, 1990). Hence, this loosely coupled, asynchronous architectural style supports flexibility, robustness, and extensibility, i.e., supports the fast adaptation and integration of applications. These advantages of loosely coupled interaction were corroborated within both academic research and industry such as database systems, software engineering, or coordination theory (Cilia et al., 2001; Gatziu et al., 1998; Mühl et al., 2006; Papadopoulos & Arbab, 1998; Sullivan & Notkin, 1992).

As mentioned above, from the perspective of a user CAIPS is similar to traditional publish/subscribe systems. Within these systems occurring events and associated notifications are strongly intertwined. CAIPS, however, decouples events and notifications by supporting a flexible association of situations (i.e., happenings of interest) and messages (i.e., the notification). For example, users of a traditional weather alerting service on the one hand may be informed about disadvantageous weather change events only. CAIPS on the other hand may provide the users with additional information such as alternative indoor recommendations.

2.4 Recommender Systems

Recommender systems provide advice to users regarding items they might be interested in. In general, personalized and non-personalized recommender system can be distinguished (Schafer et al., 1999; H. Werthner, 2008). The latter does not offer individual recommendations by involving individual user interests. An example of a non-personalized recommendation is the suggestion of products with the highest average ratings (cf. Figure 6):

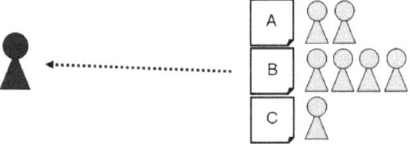

Figure 6: Non-Personalized Recommender System

Subsequently, personalized recommender systems are discussed in more detail. Personalized recommender systems make suggestions according to the users' individual preferences (Blecker et al., 2005). Hence, they support them to easily and quickly find the most valuable item by reasoning over their profiles. The profiles represent the information the recommender system *knows* about the users. Personalized recommender systems have been widely accepted and applied within e-commerce applications. Numerous of these applications have been enhanced with recommender system technologies within the last decade. A prominent representative is

2.4 Recommender Systems

Amazon.com (Amazon.com, 2008). According to Schafer et al. (1999) they enhance e-commerce sales in three ways:
- transforming website browsers into buyers
- improved cross-selling by suggesting additional products
- improving customer loyalty by creating value-added relationships between the e-commerce application and the customer

For more details concerning the relationship of recommender systems and e-commerce refer to Schafer et al. (1999; 2001). According to Burke (2002) and Zanker & Jessenitschnig (2008) personalized recommender systems are composed of the following basic components:
- *User model*: stores knowledge concerning the user; this may range from demographic data up to the user's preferences according certain items. The preferences may be acquired *explicitly* (e.g. using interactive dialogs) or *implicitly* (e.g. exploiting user ratings, or click-stream data). User profiles may be aggregated within a *community* component which provides the base for community based recommendation techniques such as collaborative and/or demographic filtering. This part of a recommender system is also known as *input data* (cf. Burke, 2002).
- *Product model*: Stores product specific information. The product model, i.e., its design and its enclosed features are heavily dependent on the recommendation strategy. Recommender systems based on collaborative filtering solely requires a unique product identifier whereas knowledge- and content-based systems require elaborate product descriptions.
- *Algorithm*: The recommendation strategy, i.e., the reasoning paradigm exploiting user, community, and product knowledge.
- *Interaction strategy*: The design of the interaction between user and recommender system. Its design is strongly influenced by the technique applied for acquiring feedback. The use of implicitly elicited user feedback, for example, click-stream data does not lead to extra effort for the user. Explicitly collected user feedback such as the rating of items, obviously, leads to additional effort for the user.

Referring to Adomavicius & Tuzhilin (2005), Balabanovic & Shoham (1997) and Burke (2002) personalized recommender systems may be classified according to their applied *recommendation strategy* as follows:
- *Knowledge-based*: Knowledge-based recommender systems suggest items based on explicit knowledge associating user and product models. Similar to knowledge-based systems in general (cf. Section 2.1) knowledge-based recommender systems also suffer

from the main drawback of such systems, namely the need for explicit knowledge representation and acquisition. Apart from that, a knowledge-based strategy offers some benefits contrasted to learn-based techniques discussed below. Among others, pure knowledge-based approaches do not suffer from the *ramp-up* problem (Konstan et al., 1998) which occurs to new users and new items of recommender systems.

Knowledge-based recommenders may be implemented using *rule and constraint techniques* such as discussed in Jannach (2004). An additional technique for implementing knowledge-based recommender systems is *case-based reasoning* (Jackson, 1999; Kolodner, 1993; Watson & Marir, 1994). Humans effectively employ memories and experiences to solve new problems, i.e., by recalling past problem solutions. Case-based reasoning (CBR) maps this human problem solving strategy to computable models. The core of each CBR system is its *case base* acting as a repository of old cases. A case acts as a container for knowledge about the problem, its context, and its solution. The essence of this approach is its capability to recognize problems similar to the current one and adapting its solution to the new one; this functionality is usually encapsulated within *retriever* and *modifier* components. A case-based recommender system in turn treats the items being recommended as cases and uses CBR for retrieving or ranking appropriate items. A common approach is that a user specifies a query by posing some restrictions concerning related features of the item being recommended. The query's result is ranked afterwards by the use of similar cases stored in the case base. Examples of this approach are discussed in Burke (Burke, 2002), Ricci & Werthner (2002), and Ricci et al. (2001). A comprehensive survey of case-based and conversational recommendations is provided by Smyth (2007).

- *Content-based*: The content-based approach is rooted in the information retrieval community (Balabanovic & Shoham, 1997). Items are recommended based on a comparison between their identifying features (cf. Figure 7):

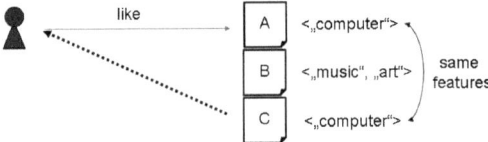

Figure 7: Content-Based Recommendation Strategy

This approach is also known as *Item to Item Correlation* (Schafer et al., 1999). Based on the features, characterizing the item a user has rated, a profile representing his interests is

2.4 Recommender Systems

created. Content-based recommender systems are usually realized as classifier systems based on machine learning research (Ricci & Werthner, 2002).

- *Collaborative*: The major advantage of collaborative systems is that they do not require an elaborate representation of the items being recommended; therefore they are well suited for the representation of complex objects. Collaborative techniques are also known as *People to People Correlation* (Schafer et al., 1999). A recommender system which applies the collaborative style suggests items that are preferred by highly correlated users (cf. Figure 8):

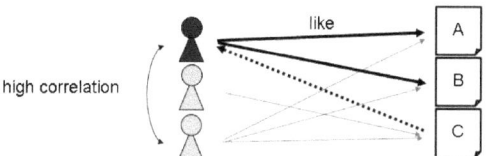

Figure 8: Collaborative Recommendation Strategy

The collaborative recommendation technique is exemplified in Figure 9:

	I 1	I 2	I 3	I 4	I 5
U 1	5	8		7	8
U 2	10		1		
U 3	2		10	9	9
U 4		2	9	9	10
U 5	1	5			1
Active User	2		9	10	X

Figure 9: Collaborative Filtering, Example

In the example above, the item "I5" is suggested to the active user because this item is preferred by the highly correlated user "U3".

Furthermore, Burke (2002) distinguishes between collaborative and demographic recommendations. Demographic ones build people to people correlations as well. However, instead of classifying users based on their ratings they are categorized based on their demographic attributes; the items are recommended according to these demographic classes (cf. Figure 10):

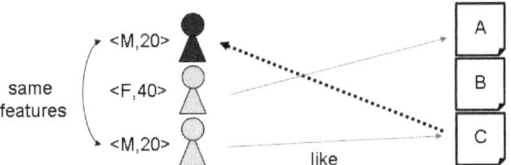

Figure 10: Demographic Based Collaborative Filtering

The strengths of the demographic based approach are the independence of historical data, i.e., they do not require a history of user ratings.

- *Hybrid approaches*: Hybrid recommendation strategies combine two or more of the base types. They enhance and complement one another aiming to overcome the shortcomings inherent to the basic recommendation strategies. For more details concerning hybrid recommendation strategies refer to Adomavicius & Tuzhilin (2005), Burke (2002) and Zanker et al. (Zanker et al., 2006).

2.4.1 Utilization within CAIPS & Discussion

CAIPS is focused on the situation dependent delivery of personalized messages. Recommender systems are a key enabling technology for creating these messages. The messages provide their recipients with suitable information regarding their current situation. For example, in tourism such a message may inform tourists about events taking place within the next few days (cf. Section 1.1.2). Based on the user's current situation and his preferences the suggested event is individually determined employing a recommender system. The case study in Section 4 is based on a specific implementation of CAIPS (CAIPS-IM) for the mobile tourist guide *innsbruck.mobile* integrating the knowledge based recommender system *CWA* (Jannach, 2004; Zanker et al., 2008).

3 Designing CAIPS

> *Everything in nature, in the inanimate as well as the animate world, happens according to rules, although we do not always know these rules. Water falls according to the laws of gravity and the locomotion of animals also takes place according to rules. The fish in the water, the bird in the air move according to rules. All nature actually is nothing but a nexus of appearances according to rules; and there is nothing at all without rules. When we believe that we have come across an absence of rules, we can only say that the rules are unknown to us.*
>
> Immanuel Kant (1724 - 1804)

This section is the central part of this thesis. It proposes the conceptual framework behind CAIPS. As already mentioned in Section 1, CAIPS denotes a system type and not a specific implementation. The conceptual framework acts as an abstract instruction guide for the design of specific systems. It is mainly composed of a *reference model* and the declarative *Context-Aware Information Triggering Language* which are discussed in sections 3.5.1 and 3.5.2 respectively. Prior to the discussion of the conceptual framework the basics are introduced: First, an overview of the approach is presented in Section 3.1. Subsequently, the involved stakeholders of CAIPS are introduced in Section 3.2. The requirements of CAIPS are specified in Section 3.3. Relevant definitions are introduced in Section 3.4.

3.1 Overview of CAIPS

Based on the objectives and requirements stated in sections 1 and 3.3 respectively, the objective of building CAIPS may be summarized as the design of a system which enables the service provider to declaratively specify the automatic sending of tailored messages to his consumers. CAIPS aims at optimizing the consumers search and complexity costs by tackling the drawbacks of *information retrieval effort* and *information overload*. Referring to Section

2.2.1 CAIPS may be regarded as a context-aware application combining two application categories, namely *contextual presentation* and *context-triggered actions*.

The issue of proactive information delivery, i.e., reducing the information retrieval effort is tackled by choosing the *push based* information dissemination approach. In general two different dissemination approaches can be distinguished, namely *push* and *pull* (Cheverst et al., 2001; Frank, 1997; Kendall & Kendall, 1999). The traditional pull approach requires that users know a priori where and when to look for information or that they spend an inordinate amount of time polling known sites for updates. Push based services, on the other hand, relieve their users from these burdens, i.e., the user is not forced to search for relevant information himself; rather, the users are proactively provided with situation dependent information. Hence, the effort for gathering information is significantly reduced (cf. Cheverst et al., 2001; Kendall & Kendall, 1999). Therefore, push based information delivery is well suited to tackle the issue of information retrieval effort. As it is not required to request new data continuously (which is also called *polling*) a permanent data connection is not necessary and therefore a waste of resources can be avoided (cf. Franklin & Zdonik, 1998). This fact is particularly important in the field of mobile, context-aware systems which are especially susceptible to resource waste because of their limited resources such as processing power and bandwidth.

The issue of information overload is addressed by providing highly personalized information, i.e., by providing exactly that information significantly relevant to the user's current situation. As discussed in Section 2.4, recommender systems provide users with personalized advices concerning items they might be interested in. Hence, they offer an excellent technique for providing personalized messages.

The specification of *what* should be sent to *whom* and *when*, i.e., the specification of the *Message Triggering Situation* and its associated *Message Type* is realized completely declarative employing the CAIPS internal rule language CAITL (cf. Section 3.5.2). The proposed rule-based approach enables to declaratively define new *Message Types* and to specify when the derived Messages should be sent. In other words, the complete message handling process may be controlled in a purely declarative way. Applying the rule-based approach leads to several advantages compared to implementing reactive behavior directly in application code such as modularity, maintainability, extensibility, and declarative specification.

The entire process of declarative context-aware information delivery considered from the perspective of a service provider, as well as the user's perspective, is summarized in Figure 11:

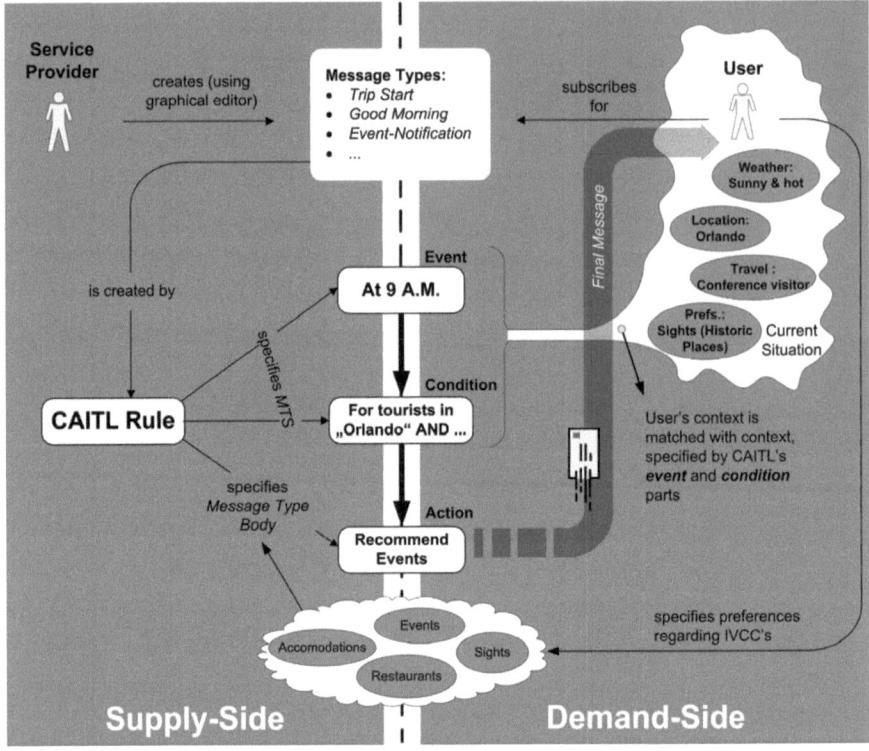

Figure 11: Overview Context-Aware Information Delivery

The focus is the exemplification of the message creation and sending process. The service provider, representing the supplier side, is illustrated on the left side. He creates *Message Types* by stating CAITL rules such as rules for the *Message Types* identified in Section 1.1.2. The service provider is supported in creating CAITL rules by a graphical editor (cf. Section 3.5.1.13). In the simplified example below he creates a rule for the "Good Morning Message" *Message Type*. The stated *Message Triggering Situation* (MTS) (cf. Section 3.4.6) leads to a selection of all users whose current situation matches the defined restrictions, i.e., all users who are located in Orlando at 9:00 A. M. are chosen (certainly, more sophisticated selection criteria could be stated, as indicated by "AND ..."). For each of these users the appropriate *Message Instance* is derived subsequently. The contained *Information Value Chain Instances* (IVCI) (cf. Section 3.4.3) are determined in a two-tiered process. First, at design-time the service provider defines the *Information Value Chain Concepts* he wants to recommend according to the specified MTS. Second, the associated *Information Value Chain Instances* are derived automatically using recommender and basic retrieval techniques. After determining the IVCI's according to the

3.2 Stakeholders

user's context and his preferences the *Final Message* is delivered to the user exploiting his preferred communication channel.

Considered from an architectural perspective the central idea behind the design of CAIPS is based on the synthesis of a number of well-known system architectures, namely those of expert, context-aware, recommender, and publish/subscribe systems. The design of CAIPS was particularly inspired by expert and context-aware systems. The role of these systems and their influence on CAIPS is described in Section 3.5.1.

Similar to rule-based expert systems the problem-solving heuristic of CAIPS is based on rules. Within CAIPS the expert knowledge is acquired through the service provider, playing the role of an expert, employing the rules to define a MTS and its associated *Message Type*. Obviously, the definition of a MTS strongly depends on contextual information which is in turn acquired using techniques known from context-aware systems. These two systems enhance each other and form the skeletal structure for embedding the remaining functional components such as those from recommender systems providing the functionalities for personalizing the IVCCs. Recommender and context-aware systems complement each other by helping users finding relevant items (Choeh & Lee, 2008; van Setten et al., 2004). The latter heavily employs the publish/subscribe paradigm for acquiring context information.

Details concerning the functional composition of CAIPS are discussed in Section 3.5.1.

3.2 Stakeholders

This thesis distinguishes between two stakeholders:

- *Service provider*: Represents the operator of CAIPS; conceives the system as an enabler to provide his consumers with tailored messages depending on their current situation. For example, in tourism a destination management organization (DMO) may act as a service provider.
- *User*: Represents the end-user of CAIPS; conceives the system as a service providing him with exactly that information he is currently interested in. A tourist, for example, represents a potential end-user of CAIPS.

3.3 Requirements Elicitation

Prior to the design of the conceptual framework of CAIPS (cf. Section 3.5) a requirements analysis was carried out. The aim of this analysis was to identify common requirements of prospective *context-aware information push systems* which have to be fulfilled by a respective conceptual framework. The underlying requirement elicitation process was based on a comprehensive survey, including scenarios (cf. Section 1.1), use cases (cf. Section 1.1.2), and early prototypes, of four potential service providers[9]. Subsequently, these service providers, which originate from different service domains, and related application scenarios are introduced:

- *Destination of Innsbruck*: The destination of Innsbruck is an urban destination located in the middle of the Alps. A consortium of representatives of the local public transport, the local city marketing, and the city government of Innsbruck act as a common potential service provider. The application scenario is to employ CAIPS as an integrated part of the city's mobile tourist guide (cf. Section 4).
- *Olympiaworld Innsbruck*: The organization *Olympiaworld Innsbruck* hosts different sport facilities and event venues. It is among the most important event centers in Austria, for example, three matches of the EURO 2008 took place in facilities of the *Olympiaworld Innsbruck*. A corresponding application scenario regarding CAIPS is the notification of potential visitors about suitable events or occurring traffic jams.
- *Österreichisches Verkehrsbüro AG*: The *Verkehrsbüro Group* is Austria's biggest tourism group focusing on hotel industry and tourism. A corresponding application scenario

---

[9] The requirements elicitation process took place within the development of the etPlanner framework in 2006 (Höpken et al., 2006).

regarding CAIPS is to provide end-users with information concerning their upcoming travel such as personalized destination information or hotel related information.
- *Dolomiti Superski*: Dolomiti Superski is a skiing destination situated in South Tirol, Italy. With more than 1100 km of skiing slopes it belongs to the largest skiing regions of Europe. A corresponding application scenario regarding CAIPS is to provide skiing-related information such as weather forecasts or skiing huts.

Subsequently, the results, i.e., the elicited functional requirements[10] are specified. They are classified according to the involved stakeholders (cf. Section 3.2):

Service Provider Requirements:

SP-Req.-1 *Automatic Message Delivery*: The system's fundamental feature is the *automatic* delivery of messages triggered by the occurrence of certain situations.

SP-Req.-2 *Situation Dependent Message Content Definition:* The content of a message must be specifiable depending on the triggering situation.

SP-Req.-3 *Automatic Personalization*: A message must be automatically personalized according to its receiver's profile.

SP-Req.-4 *Extensibility:* The system must support to add new messages and to easily embed them in the overall architecture.

SP-Req.-5 *Ease-of-use:* The system should be easily applicably by typical office employees with no strong background in information technology.

SP-Req.-6 *Multiple Communication Channels*: The system must support several communication channels.

User requirements:

U-Req.-1 *Expressive Subscription Specification*: The user must be enabled to expressively specify his information needs, i.e., to specify the information he wants to automatically receive.

U-Req.-2 *Practical Subscription Interfaces*: The system must provide subscription interfaces for the most popular mobile and stationary devices.

U-Req.-3 *Avoid Similar Message Content*: The system must avoid spamming, i.e., the user must not receive the same messages several times.

---

[10] The identified non-functional requirements such as heterogeneous platform support or the minimization of license costs were omitted because they did not directly affect the design of the conceptual framework

3.4 Definitions

This section introduces fundamental terms aiming at facilitating the read- and understandability of subsequent sections.

3.4.1 Message Type

The skeletal structure of a message[11] is specified by its *Message Type*. From the perspective of the service provider a *Message Type* represents a message he may offer to his users. From the user's perspective a *Message Type* represents a channel (cf. Section 2.3.2.3) he may subscribe to if he is interested in the kind of information provided by this channel.

A *Message Type* is composed of two fundamental components, namely the *Message Type Body* and the *Message Type Metadata*. The former acts as a container storing conceptual data about arbitrary *Information Value Chain Concepts* (cf. Section 3.4.3). Its design is illustrated in Figure 13.

The latter stores *Message Type* specific metadata such as a label or a general description. Metadata are applied across all derived *Message Instances* (cf. Section 3.4.4), whereas the body is computed for each *Message Instance* (cf. Section 3.4.4) individually.

A *Message Type* is implicitly created at rule design time, i.e., when a new rule is created. Its design is summarized in Figure 12:

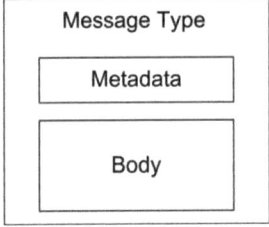
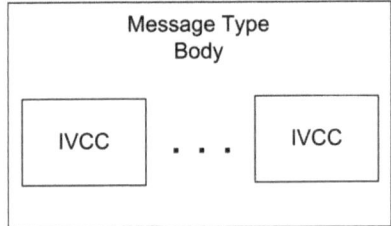

Figure 12: Message Type   Figure 13: Message Type Body

3.4.2 Information Value Chain Concept

As far as knowledge representation theory is concerned an *Information Value Chain Concept* (IVCC) may be put on a level with a *concept* indicating the category of the objects being represented. Concepts (or types) represent abstract specifications not sets of things. For every type t there is a set δt called the denotation of t (Brachman & Levesque, 2004; Sowa, 2000). δt is

---

[11] To facilitate the read- and understandability the term message is used; however, its exact meaning is refined in section 3.4.5

built by listing all possible instances of *t*. In this thesis the term *concept* is used when talking about *t*.

Strongly related to concepts and types is the definition of *intensional* and *extensional* knowledge (Brachman & Levesque, 2004; Sowa, 2000). These terms were initially used in the field of *terminological knowledge representation* which is also known as *concept description language* and *concept language*. These terms emphasizes the relationship between intensional knowledge and concepts which are mainly used to build terminologies or taxonomies, which in turn are typical representatives of intensional knowledge. Intensional knowledge specifies the properties or criteria for recognizing instances without their possible existence, i.e., it represents the general knowledge about a domain of discourse.

As discussed in Rasinger et al. (2006), an *information value chain element* represents intensional as well as extensional knowledge about a specific destination product. Based on this notation an *Information Value Chain Concept* is defined as an *information value chain element* storing intensional knowledge exclusively. Example IVCCs are concepts defining intensional knowledge about sights, events, or a destination's weather.

3.4.3 Information Value Chain Instance

Corresponding to an *Information Value Chain Concept* an *Information Value Chain Instance* (IVCI) represents restricted extensional knowledge. Usually, extensional knowledge (also known as the denotation) is built by listing all possible instances of a specific concept (Donini et al., 1991; Sowa, 2000). Therefore, the term *restricted* extensional knowledge is used to point out that only those instances are chosen which perfectly match a user's context and preferences. For example, the "Hofburg in Innsbruck" (because the respective user is interested in historical sights and is currently staying in Innsbruck) or the weather forecast for the user's current location are typical representatives of IVCIs.

3.4.4 Message Instance

A *Message Instance* stores user specific instances of an *Information Value Chain Concept*, i.e., *Information Value Chain Instances*. For each IVCC contained in a *Message Type Body* the appropriate user specific instance is derived at runtime. In addition to IVCIs a *Message Instance* may also store user and explanation specific data such as a receiver's name, his mobile number, or explanatory data. The latter may be exploited to explain the user why he has received the message (i.e., the contained IVCIs). The design of a *Message Instance* is illustrated in Figure 14:

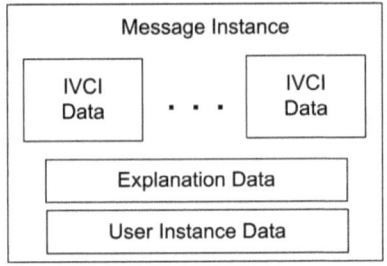

Figure 14: Design of Message Instance

3.4.5 Final Message

A *Final Message* acts as a container for a rendered *Message Instance*. For each of a user's preferred communication channels a *Final Message* is rendered based on the corresponding *Message Instance*. A *Final Message* may be regarded as the final product conveyed to the user.

The relationship between *Message Type*, *Message Instance*, and *Final Message* is summarized in Figure 15 and Figure 16:

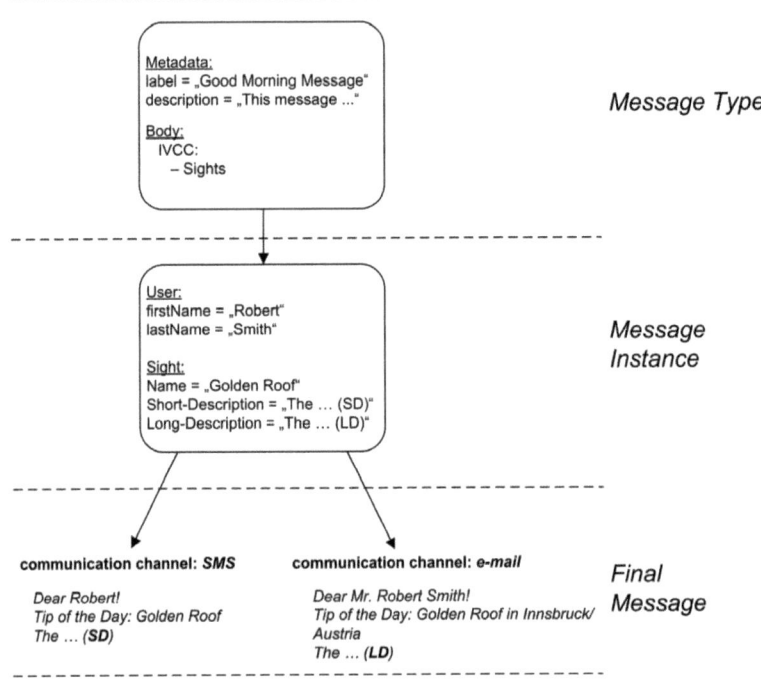

Figure 15: Message Type, Message Instance, Final Message

3.5 Conceptual Framework

The example in Figure 15 illustrates that due to the limited number of allowed characters a SMS message contains a short description (SD) of the corresponding sight only whereas the E-Mail message contains a detailed description (LD) of the appropriate sight as well as the user's full name.

Figure 16 illustrates that a *Message Instance* is derived from the corresponding *Message Type* for each user (U) individually at runtime. Each *Final Message* in turn is rendered according to the user's desired communication channel(s) (CC).

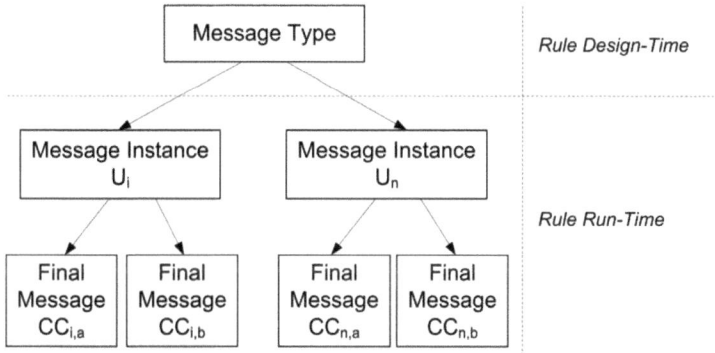

Figure 16: 1 Message Type – n Message Instances – n Final Messages

3.4.6 Message Triggering Situation

A *Message Triggering Situation* (MTS) describes the situation whose occurrence triggers the message creation and sending process for all users currently in this situation. This situation is defined by the event and condition part of the *Context-Aware Information Triggering Language* (cf. Section 3.5.2). A *Message Triggering Situation* may be considered as an extension of the *situation abstraction* concept proposed by Henricksen (2004). While the latter focuses on further raising the abstraction level of context information the MTS may be regarded as a higher abstraction level consisting of arbitrary such combined situations.

3.4.7 Duplicate Message

A *Duplicate Message* denotes a *Final Message* sent to the same user multiple times caused by his multiple passing of the same *Message Triggering Situation*.

3.5 Conceptual Framework

This section introduces the conceptual framework which aims to facilitate the design and implementation of specific context-aware information push systems such as CAIPS-IM (cf. Section 4). It is fundamentally composed of a *reference model* and a *rule language framework*.

The former defines the fundamental functional/logical parts of context-aware push systems (cf. Section 3.5.1). The latter provides a framework supporting the development of a corresponding rule language (cf. Section 3.5.2) enabling to control the complete messaging process through rules.

3.5.1 Reference Model

This section describes the reference model of CAIPS. First, the role of the reference model as employed within this thesis is discussed. Subsequently, the derivation of the constituting entities from the corresponding base systems (cf. Section 2) as well as their functionalities are described.

In general, a reference model decomposes a known problem into parts that cooperatively solve that problem. It specifies a minimal set of unifying entities and their relationships within a particular problem domain. A reference model is not directly tied to any technologies or other concrete implementation details (Bass et al., 2003; MacKenzie et al., 2006).

Within this thesis the reference model can be considered as an abstract framework defining the fundamental functional entities of CAIPS as well as their relationships. It decomposes the problem domain of context-aware information push systems into entities cooperatively meeting the related objectives and requirements (cf. sections 1 and 3.3 respectively).

The reference model aims to fulfill the following tasks:

- Identify the functional elements that are common in context-aware push systems
- Provide an abstract framework for understanding significant entities and relationships between them
- Capture communication and dependencies among the functional elements in context-aware push systems
- Support the implementation of specific context-aware information push systems. For example, *innsbruck.mobile* was designed and implemented based on this reference model (cf. Section 4).
- Provide a common terminology employable unambiguously across different implementations

The reference model is presented as a diagram comprising the fundamental involved functional/logical entities as well as their interaction in Figure 17. In order to improve readability add-on functionality providing entities as well as the corresponding user interfaces were not included. Nonetheless, they are briefly described in Section 3.5.1.12 and Section 3.5.1.13 respectively.

3.5 Conceptual Framework

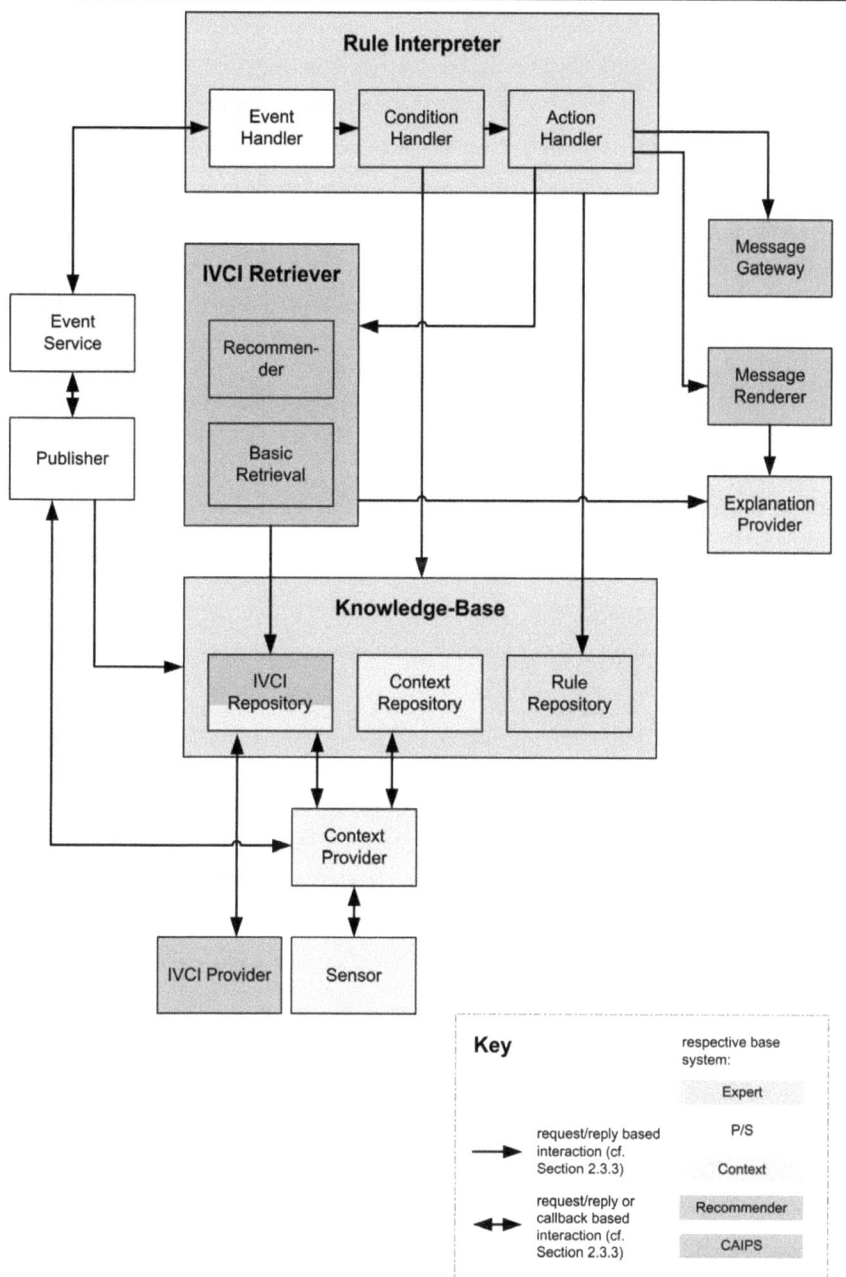

Figure 17: CAIPS – Reference Model

The design of the reference model was fundamentally driven by base systems introduced in Section 2, namely expert, context-aware, publish/subscribe, and recommender systems. Some of the constituent entities can be directly related to appropriate entities of these systems. However, the functional elements required for CAIPS can not be entirely covered by these derived entities only. Furthermore, the reference model is composed of CAIPS specific entities which can not be related to the base systems as well. Subsequently, the entities constituting the reference model are discussed, .i.e., their responsibilities are described and the respective base system's counterpart is identified (if possible). To emphasize the relationship between the base systems studied in Section 2 and the reference model, its entities are colored according to the appropriate counterpart of the corresponding base system.

3.5.1.1 Knowledge-Base

As described in Section 2.1.3, expert systems store their complete problem solving knowledge within a central component, i.e., within the knowledge-base. Similarly, one of the fundamental concepts of CAIPS is its knowledge-based problem solving approach. The corresponding problem solving knowledge, i.e., the knowledge for declaratively and proactively sending tailored messages, is explicitly and centrally organized within a *Knowledge-Base*.

The *Knowledge-Base* stores both declarative and procedural knowledge (cf. Section 3.5.2.1). It is separated into three parts, namely the *IVCI Repository*, the *Context Repository*, and the *Rule Repository*.

The *IVCI Repository* stores IVCI relevant information. The stored IVCI specific information is primarily exploited by the *IVCI Retrieval* entity (cf. Section 3.5.1.3). However, under certain circumstances this repository may also contain contextual information as there is a seamless transition between these two. For example, common information regarding sights such as their descriptions can be considered as typical IVCI specific information; however, their opening times may also be considered as contextual information. This relation is illustrated in Figure 18:

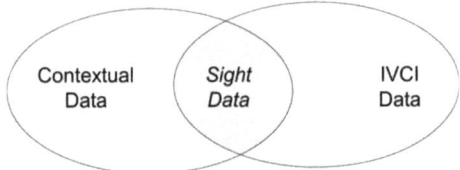

Figure 18: Context and IVCI Data

The *Context Repository* is equivalent to the homonymous component of context-aware systems (cf. Section 2.2.2). It acts as a user-centric repository for storing context information comprising both intensional and extensional knowledge. In addition to current, historical context information is stored as well[12].

The *Rule Repository* provides a central repository for storing the CAITL rules (cf. Section 3.5.2) as well as rule related metadata such as its creation timestamp, whether it is active, or the rule author. They are maintained by the service provider utilizing a high-level rule editor facilitating the rule creation process (cf. Section 3.5.1.13).

The *Rule Repository*, i.e., the contained rules together with the intensional part of the *Knowledge-Base* may be compared to the expert systems' heuristic component, and the extensional part to the case-specific knowledge component (cf. Section 2.1.3).

3.5.1.2 Rule Interpreter

As described in Section 2.1, knowledge-based and expert systems are fundamentally composed of a knowledge-base and an appropriate inference engine. Similarly, the fundamental building block of CAIPS in addition to its *Knowledge-Base* is the corresponding inference engine. CAIPS' *Knowledge-Base* stores declarative as well as procedural knowledge. The latter is represented exploiting customized E-C-A rules (cf. Section 3.5.2). Consequently, the inference engine's equivalent is a *Rule Interpreter* responsible for interpreting these rules.

Its core functionality is provided by three parts complementing one another, namely the *Event Handler*, the *Condition Handler*, and the *Action Handler*.

The publish/subscribe communication paradigm is well suited for realizing the interpretation of a rule's event part as it is designed to directly reflect the intrinsic behavior of information-driven applications (Mühl, 2002; Mühl et al., 2006). The *Event Handler* may be compared to a *consumer* component in publish/subscribe systems (cf. Section 2.3.2). It provides the counterpart to the *Publisher* (cf. Section 3.5.1.5) on the other side of the communication path. It exploits a rule's event part to state its interest in certain notifications by issuing and passing an appropriate subscription to the *Event Service* (cf. Section 3.5.1.6). In case of a successful subscription, i.e., if the *Event Service* has successfully matched a subscription and has forwarded a notification, the *Event Handler* transforms and binds the notification to an internal representation structure (cf. Section 3.5.2.5). Afterwards it triggers the *Condition Handler* to evaluate the rule's condition part.

---

[12] It is worth noting that it may be differentiated between static and dynamic contextual information. The former is stored in the *Context Repository*, the latter is provided by the *Publisher* component exploiting notifications.

The *Condition Handler* transforms the rule's condition definition into the appropriate query language and delegates the query processing to the related query engine. In case of a successful query, i.e., if one or more users were found meeting the restrictions, the *Condition Handler* binds these results to an internal representation structure (cf. Section 3.5.2.5).

The *Action Handler* is responsible for creating the appropriate *Message Instance* as well as for producing and sending the derived *Final Message(s)*. The *Message Instance*, i.e., the contained IVCIs is determined exploiting an *ICVI Retrieval* entity (cf. Section 3.5.1.3). Subsequently, the *Final Message* is created and delivered drawing on the *Message Renderer* (cf. Section 3.5.1.9) and *Message Gateway* (cf. Section 3.5.1.10) entities.

This process including a description of the interaction between the rule engine's components is described in more detail in Sections 3.5.2.3 and 3.5.2.6 respectively.

3.5.1.3 IVCI Retrieval

A *Message Instance* is composed of a number of *Information Value Chain Instances*. Such an *IVCI* is determined for every user individually using recommender and/or basic retrieval mechanisms. This functionality is encapsulated within two corresponding entities, namely a *Recommender* and a *Basic Retrieval* module. These enable the personalized retrieval of IVCIs dependent on the user's context and his preferences.

As its name implies the *Recommender* is responsible for retrieving personalized IVCIs, i.e., it determines the IVCI most valuable for the user considering his current situation as well as his preferences regarding the respective IVCC. For example, the *Recommender* module is responsible for determining the sight well suited for the user's current situation and its preferences regarding sights. For details concerning different types of recommenders and their functionalities it is referred to Section 2.4.

In addition to the elaborate, recommendation based retrieval of IVCIs the *Basic Retrieval* module supports the retrieval of IVCIs by stating restrictions on the respective IVCC. The restrictions are expressed exploiting standard query languages. The *Basic Retrieval* entity is intended for the retrieval of IVCIs which do not require an elaborate personalization process such as determining the today's weather forecast corresponding to the user's current location.

3.5.1.4 Explanation Provider

This part encapsulates the functionality for providing the user with explanations regarding the received messages. As described in Section 2.1.3, enriching the results, provided by expert systems, with explanations increases the user's confidence in using such systems. Similarly, enriching the *Final Message* with explanations may raise the acceptance of context-aware

3.5 Conceptual Framework

information push systems. A corresponding explanation is composed of two fundamental information pieces:

- description of the user's current situation explaining why the message was sent at this particular time (this information, .i.e., information explaining the MTS is provided by the *Rule Interpreter*, cf. Section 3.5.1.2)
- explanation of the proposed IVCIs (this information is provided by the *IVCI Retrieval*, i.e., the *Recommender* and/or the *Basic Retrieval* modules, cf. Section 3.5.1.3). For details concerning rule-based explanations within a knowledge-based recommender system refer to Jannach (2004).

3.5.1.5 Publisher

As described in Section 2.3, the fundamental components of a publish/subscribe system are the interacting producer and consumer components as well as the event notification service for mediating between these two. The appropriate counterparts of CAIPS are the *Event Handler* (cf. Section 3.5.1.2), the *Publisher*, and the *Event Service* (cf. Section 3.5.1.6) respectively.

Similar to the producer component of a publish/subscribe system (cf. Section 2.3) the *Publisher* is responsible for reporting happenings of interest to the mediating *Event Service* (cf. Section 3.5.1.6). CAIPS distinguishes internal and external events. The former represents the detection of happenings "inside" CAIPS such as the occurrence of a specific point of time published by a timer component. The latter represents happenings published by *Context Providers* (cf. Section 3.5.1.7) such as if a user reaches a certain location. Both functionalities, i.e., services for detecting internal events as well as a wrapper for events published by a *Context Provider* are encapsulated within the *Publisher* component. The interaction between these two components may be based on a request/reply as well as an event-based publish/subscribe interaction style (cf. Section 2.3.3).

3.5.1.6 Event Service

As mentioned in Section 3.5.1.5, the *Event Service* may be compared to the event notification service component of a publish/subscribe system. It decouples the *Publisher* and the *Event Handler* according to the three dimensions time, space, and synchronization (cf. Section 2.3.2.4). Therefore, it has to offer services for the mediation between the two interacting components such as services for storage, management, and the efficient delivery of notifications. The *Event Service* is responsible for testing incoming notifications (received from the *Publisher*) for matching subscriptions (got from the *Event Handler*) and to forward successfully matched notifications to the respective *Event Handler*.

3.5.1.7 Context Provider

As described in Section 2.2, the design of context-aware systems may be described exploiting four layers. The *Context Provider* is responsible for covering the functionalities residing on the preprocessing layer of such systems (cf. Section 2.2.2). It provides high-level contexts exploiting services for interpreting, transforming, and aggregating raw level sensor data. High-level contexts are created by interpreting low level context data, for example, determining a user's location through the mapping of his RFID chip to his personal id as implemented in the *intelligent location based information* (*ilbi*) project (ilbi, 2008). The interaction with the corresponding sensors may be based on a request/reply as well as an event-based publish/subscribe interaction style (cf. Section 2.3.3). As mentioned above, it has to be distinguished between static and dynamic contextual information. The acquisition of both contextual information types is based on the *Context-Provider*.

3.5.1.8 Sensor

The *Sensor* is responsible for covering the functionalities residing on the retrieval layer of context-aware systems (cf. Section 2.2.2).

It is responsible for acquiring low-level context information. As discussed in Section 2.2.2, physical, virtual, and logical sensors may be distinguished. In practice, sensing context information is a complex task which is accomplished by a number of separated components.

3.5.1.9 Message Renderer

The *Message Renderer* is responsible for creating the *Final Message* depending on the respective *Message Instance*. It provides the functionality for rendering a *Message Instance* according to the user's required communication channel(s). This process as well as the relationship between *Message Instance* and *Final Message* is illustrated in Section 3.4.5.

3.5.1.10 Message Gateway

The *Message Gateway* is responsible for delivering the *Final Message* to the corresponding recipient. It provides functionalities such as connecting external gateway services, transforming messages into the appropriate format (depending on the applied communication channel), and for routing the messages to the appropriate external gateway services.

3.5.1.11 IVCI Provider

An *IVCI Provider* is responsible for the integration of IVCI specific data. It provides services for interpreting, transforming, importing, or synchronizing IVCI data.

3.5 Conceptual Framework

3.5.1.12 Add-On Services

In addition to the core functionality, i.e., the declarative, context-aware delivery of personalized messages, covered by the previously introduced entities additional value adding services are required. Such value adding services, for example, provide services for message tracing or for simulating the sending process.

3.5.1.13 User Interfaces

Generally, user interfaces for both in Section 3.2 identified stakeholders, namely the service provider and the user have to be provided. Compared to expert systems the service provider plays the role of an expert; from a functional point of view the expert requires three types of user interfaces.

- Rule creation: Such an interface supports the service provider in creating the CAITL rules (cf. Section 3.5.2). It facilitates the rule creation process by relieving the user of being forced to use the rule language directly. A possible design and implementation approach which is based on the *query by forms* technique (Halpin, 2001) is discussed in Section 4.3.2.2.
- Recommender configuration & maintenance: Such an interface enables the configuration of the underlying recommender system such as the maintenance of filtering rules in knowledge-based recommenders. A graphical interface for stating filtering rules in a knowledge-based recommender employing a context-sensitive editor is proposed in Jannach (2004).
- Accessing add-on services: Provide high-level access for add-on services such as searching message logs or monitoring the sending process

The user side requires a number of interfaces as well:

- Message Subscription: Such an interface allows the user to subscribe to preferred *Message Types* and for stating additional subscription information such as preferred individual sending times.
- Preference Elicitation: Such an interface allows the user to state preferences regarding certain IVCCs (required, if exploiting explicit elicitation within a knowledge-based recommender).
- Message Delivery: Interface for the delivery of *Final Messages*. Depending on the applied communication channel they may range from traditional SMS or e-mail interfaces to midlets providing enhanced messaging features.

This is a functional classification only, therefore, this is not to say that the interfaces provided to the user must follow this separation.

3.5.2 Context-Aware Information Triggering Language (CAITL)

One of the fundamental ideas of CAIPS is to control the complete message handling process through rules. This approach enables the provider to declaratively create *Message Types* (cf. Section 3.4.1) and associate them with *Message Triggering Situations* (cf. Section 3.4.6) using rules. These rules are expressed exploiting a *context-aware information triggering language* (CAITL). CAITL is not a classical rule language by itself; it is rather a modular language framework supporting the development of specific CAITL languages.

However, before discussing details of this rule language framework its theoretical foundations concerning knowledge representation theory are analyzed.

3.5.2.1 Combining Knowledge Representations

This section briefly introduces the approach of designing CAITL from the perspective of knowledge representation theory. The employed knowledge representation technologies are motivated and the rationale for the need of combining these technologies is presented. A citation of Marvin Minsky (AAAI, 2008) serves as a starting point for further discussion:

> *Students frequently asked, "Which kind of representation is best?" and I usually replied that we'd need more research. ... But now I would reply: To solve really hard problems, we'll have to use several different representations. This is because each particular kind of data structure has its own virtues and deficiencies, and none by itself would seem adequate for all the different functions involved with what we call common sense.*

CAIPS makes heavy use of theories known from knowledge representation and knowledge engineering. A fundamental requirement all knowledge-based systems have in common is their need for a solid and detailed representation of their problem domains. As discussed in Section 2.1, the representation of the universe of discourse regarding CAIPS requires the representation of two different information types, namely declarative and procedural knowledge. An obvious approach to express knowledge related to these different information types is to employ an appropriate knowledge representation technology for each of these types. Each KR technology has its strengths and weaknesses which would be inherited by an appropriate knowledge-based system if such a system would be restricted to only a single knowledge representation technology (Dastani et al., 2008). Hence, the combination of KR technologies enables systems which exploit two or more KR technologies to benefit from the strengths of all integrated technologies (Yen et al., 1989). Marvin Minky (1986) stated in his seminal work "*The society of mind*" the need of combining at least two kind of *descriptions*, i.e., knowledge representation technologies. He argued for the combination of *structural* ("*for recognizing chairs when we see*

3.5 Conceptual Framework

them") and *functional* ("*in order to know what we can do with chairs*") descriptions to build intelligent agents. His usage of the terms structural and functional description could be compared to the terms declarative and procedural knowledge as discussed in Section 2.1.

Within CAIPS mainly two representation technologies complementing each other are employed:

- *object-oriented* or *ontology based* KR for capturing the declarative knowledge of the problem domain, i.e., for representing and storing context information
- *rules* for representing the procedural knowledge of CAIPS. As an example, from a service provider's perspective the simplified process of context-aware information delivery may be illustrated using the following conditional clause:

Message-Triggering-Situation occurs →
create and send personalized message

These rules are specified employing the *Context-Aware Information Triggering Language* (CAITL). Its design is explained in detail in the subsequent sections.

3.5.2.2 CAITL: Modular Framework

CAITL is based on the event-condition-action (E-C-A) rule paradigm. Approaches based on the E-C-A paradigm have in common that they employ three-parted rules for specifying reactivity. Due to their well-defined execution semantics and their separation into self-contained units E-C-A rules are intuitive to understand. The general meaning of an E-C-A rule is: "*when an event occurs, evaluate the condition and if it holds, execute the corresponding action*". Hence, E-C-A rules are well suited for specifying reactivity within CAIPS, i.e., to describe contextual situations which trigger the sending of interdependent information.

CAITL exploits self-contained component languages such as subscription (e.g., *A-MEDIAS*, cf. Hinze, 2003) and query languages (e.g., SQL) to specify the respective rule parts, namely the event, condition, and action part. To guarantee a seamless integration into the conceptual framework CAITL has to support heterogeneous component languages. The conceptual framework acts as an instruction guide aiming to facilitate the rapid implementation of context-aware push systems without imposing specific implementation technologies. Due to the strong relationship between the applied technologies and the rule's component languages (e.g., the dependence between the implementation of the *Knowledge-Base* (cf. Section 3.5.1.1) and the applied query language) CAITL has to support arbitrary component languages and must not be restricted to a specific one. Therefore, inspired by work from Alferes et al. (2005) and May et al. (2005a) CAITL is designed as a *modular framework* enabling to compose arbitrary component languages. The framework separates the well known generic E-C-A semantics from the individual semantics of the employed component languages, hence, ensuring a high flexibility concerning the potential component languages. This allows the specification of CAITL rules employing heterogeneous component languages (i.e., different subscription, query, and configuration languages) for specifying the corresponding event, condition, and action part.

The modular framework design is illustrated in Figure 19 drawing on a UML class diagram:

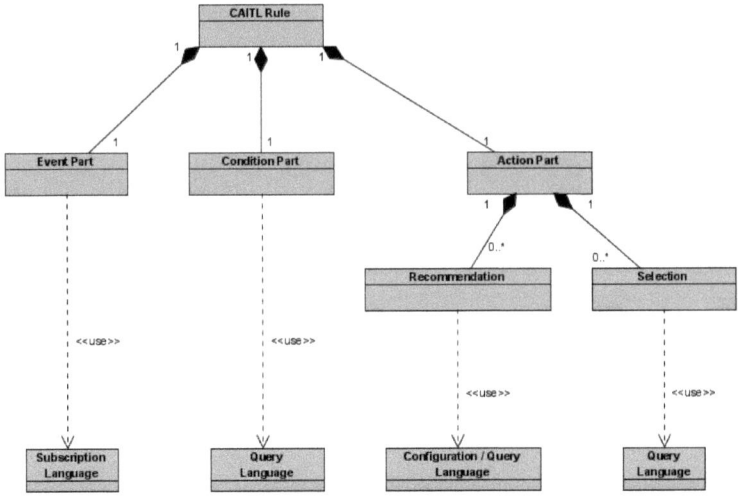

Figure 19: CAITL Rule Parts

This modular framework leads to a number of advantages:

- CAITL is independent of the applied context modeling approach, i.e., the implementation of the context-repository (cf. Sections 3.5.1.1 and 4.1) is not restricted to certain modeling and representation techniques
- The expressiveness for specifying the *Message Triggering Situation* (which depends on the expressiveness of the component languages applied for specifying a rule's event and condition part, cf. Section 3.4.6) may be customized to each problem domain individually by employing appropriate component languages
- The *application development barrier* (Henricksen & Indulska, 2004) may be reduced as each developer may choose his preferred component languages

3.5.2.3 CAITL: Global Semantics

The semantics of common E-C-A rules cover a variety of reactive application types (Papamarkos et al., 2004). E-C-A rules are also well qualified for specifying reactivity within CAIPS, i.e., to describe contextual situations which trigger the sending of interdependent

3.5 Conceptual Framework

information. For this purpose, however, the global semantics of the general E-C-A rule paradigm has to be adapted to the specific characteristics of CAIPS. CAITL distinguishes between global and local semantics (cf. Behrends et al., 2006). The former specifies the overall meaning of a CAITL rule, i.e., the way a CAITL rule is interpreted according to its constituent parts, namely its event, condition, and action part. The latter is inherently provided by the corresponding component languages. CAITL's global semantics is described below.

Similar to conventional E-C-A rules the rule execution in CAITL is triggered by the occurrence of some event (primitive or composite, cf. Section 2.3.4), i.e., each rule which denotes its interest in this kind of event is scheduled for further processing. A rule's interest in any kind of event is expressed through a subscription statement which in turn must be specified in the corresponding subscription language (cf. Section 2.3.4). As already mentioned above, CAITL supports different subscription languages which define the local semantics of the rule's event part.

The condition part of each successfully subscribed rule is evaluated in the next step, i.e., the predicate which must be satisfied to execute a rule's action part is evaluated. The condition is expressed as a truth valued query exploiting standard query languages[13]; it is interpreted as a truth value if the query's result is non empty. The query is used to restrict the potential message receivers by posing restrictions upon the corresponding context repository (cf. Section 3.5.1.1). The term *restrictions* is used according to the *restriction operator* known from relational algebra (cf. Codd, 1970; Date, 2004). CAITL strongly pursues a *user-centric* approach, i.e., the query may involve any other concept of the context model which is related (cf. join in relational databases, or predicates in RDF, cf. McBride, 2004; Powers, 2003) to the user concept. One consequence arising from the user-centric approach is that the result of a CAITL condition evaluation (i.e., the result of the corresponding query statement) has to return instances of the user concept. The term *concept* is consciously used instead of implementation dependent notations such as *table* or *class* to emphasize the independence of the applied query language from the implementation of the context repository. After completing the condition evaluation it is certain whether a *Message Triggering Situation* (cf. Section 3.4.6) has occurred or not. Also, the user(s) whose current situation matches the predefined contextual state were determined.

The rule's action part is responsible for creating and sending the *Final Message* (cf. Section 3.4.5). First, the appropriate *Message Instance* (cf. Section 3.4.4) is created for each of the previously determined message receivers depending on their context and their individual

---

[13] Similar to the event part CAITL supports arbitrary query languages

preferences. Therefore, the corresponding IVCIs are determined by evaluating the employed component languages[14]. As described in Section 3.5.1.3, CAIPS supports two mechanisms for situation dependent retrieval of *Information Value Chain Instances*, namely recommendation and basic retrieval techniques. These two retrieval mechanisms are supported by the appropriate component languages. The former exploits recommender specific query (cf. RQL proposed by Adomvicius & Tuzhilin, 2001) and configuration languages (cf. CWA-CL described in Section 4.2). The latter is based on standard query languages and supports the "direct" retrieval of IVCIs. Both techniques enable a personalized retrieval of IVCIs depending on the user's current situation and his preferences. Contrasted to the event and condition part the action part is not solely specified by the applied component languages. Rather, it inherently contains pure computational tasks, namely the creation of the *Final Message* and its delivery to the corresponding recipient.

The interpretation of a rule as well as the relationship between rule design and execution time is summarized in Figure 20:

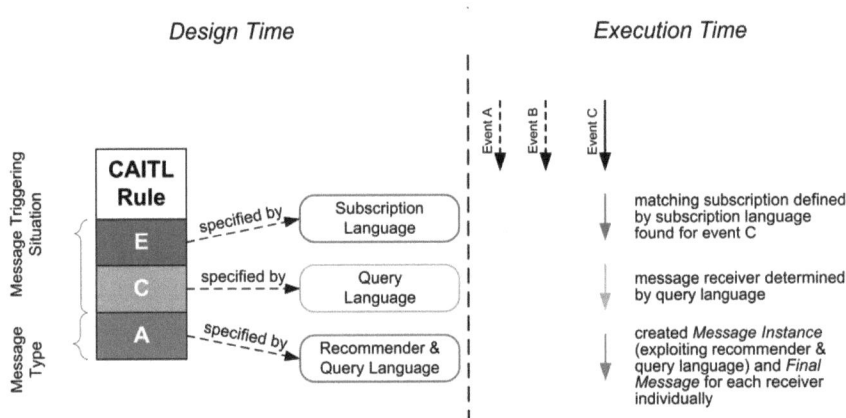

Figure 20: CAITL Rule Definition & Execution

Finally, it is worth noting that the proposed approach does not require an analysis of the rule behavior by the means of analyzing whether one rule may mutually trigger another one which may lead to unexpected rule executions as discussed in Bailey et al. (2002) and Baralis et al. (1998). In general, two cases have to be distinguished when analyzing unexpected rule behavior (cf. James Bailey et al., 2002):

---

[14] It is worth noting that the message type body (cf. Section 3.4.1) is implicitly defined at rule design time by specifying the rule's action part

3.5 Conceptual Framework

- *Triggering Relation*: A rule r_i may trigger a rule r_j if execution of r_i's action generates an event which in turn triggers rule r_j.
- *Activation Relation*: A rule r_i may activate a rule r_j if the condition of r_j may be changed from false to true based on the execution of r_i's action.

Only the second case is relevant for CAIPS. As described above the semantics of a CAITL's action part is focused on creating *Final Messages*. The action part's semantics does not foresee a possibility to fire new events, i.e., to declaratively create new events. Therefore, within CAITL a rule can not trigger another rule directly and unexpected rule behavior caused by such a *triggering relation* does not have to be considered.

Unexpected rule behavior based on an *activation relation* deals with the unexpected execution of rules caused by a rule's action part changing another rule's condition from false to true. As described above, the condition within CAITL is specified as a truth valued query against the *context repository* (cf. Sections 3.5.1.1 and 4.1). Thus, a condition solely changes from false to true if the state of the underlying repository has been changed. CAITL does not support the direct, explicit modification of the corresponding *Knowledge-Base* (i.e., of the *Context Repository*). The repository may be modified in an indirect style, e.g., by storing each user's received messages. This in turn may affect the evaluation of a rule's condition part if it includes restrictions concerning the user's already received messages. This is the only scenario within CAIPS where unexpected rule behavior due to an *activation relation* may occur. However, this case may be neglected as this scenario does not represent unexpected rule behavior; it rather represents a "desired" behavior exploited, for example, to avoid sending *Duplicate Messages* (cf. Section 3.4.7).

The proposed approach does not support the prioritization of rules, i.e., if the same event is exploited by several rules, no specific rule execution order can be defined. However, as proposed by Bonifati (2001) such a functionality could be easily integrated.

3.5.2.4 CAITL: Syntax

As discussed in the previous section, CAITL distinguishes between global and local semantics. CAITL's syntax, accordingly, supports both by providing a "global" markup which enables the direct embedding of component languages based on their native syntax. The global markup reflects CAITL's global semantics and represents the invariant section of a CAITL rule. Similar to work provided by Alferes et al. (2005), XML is employed to markup this invariant part of a CAITL rule.

The corresponding XML markup, which, among other things, aims to support computation by an appropriate rule engine is introduced subsequently. The fundamental structure of a CAITL rule was already introduced in Section 3.5.2.2. This structure is mapped to an adequate XML based representation which is sketched in Figure 21:

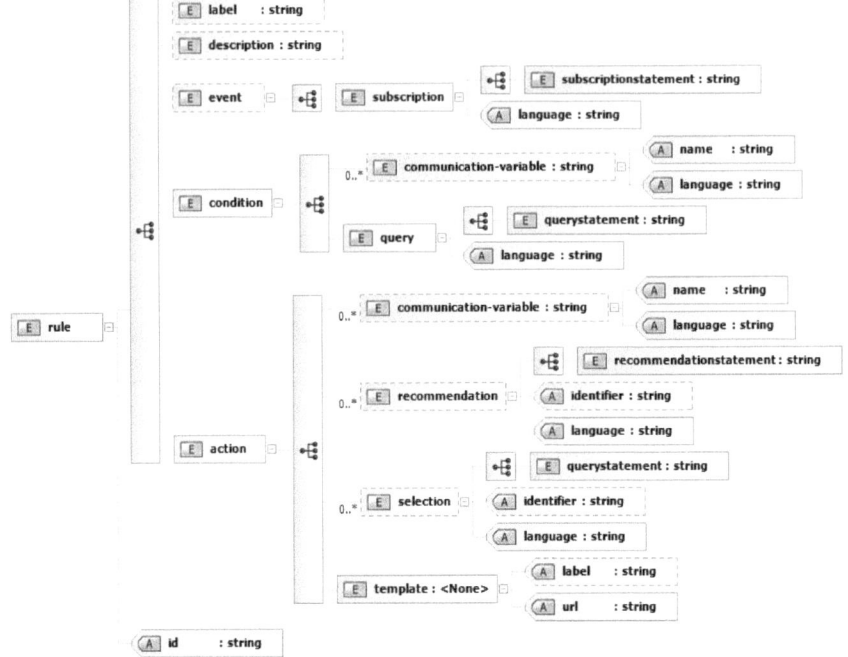

Figure 21: CAITL Rule – XML Representation

The fundamental syntactic building blocks of a CAITL rule are the `event`, `condition`, and `action` element. In addition to these constituting elements a syntactically valid rule, additionally, has to specify some metadata using the `label` and the `description` element as well as the `id` attribute. Each of the three constituting elements (`event`, `condition`, and `action`) provides an element for embedding the proprietary component language statement drawing on the following elements:

- `subscription`
- `query`
- `recommendation`
- `selection`

These elements cover the native component language statements exploiting a corresponding `statement` element (cf. `subscription`, `query`, `recommendation`, and `selectionstatement`) and a `language` attribute. The `statement` element contains the

3.5 Conceptual Framework

instruction statement of the associated component language which is specified in the corresponding native syntax; the `language` identifies the underlying component language. Within the action's `recommendation` and `selection` element the `identifier` attribute may be specified to support the binding of the corresponding results when creating the *Final Message* as well as for specifying the *Message Type Body*. Additionally, the action element must provide template related information using the `template` element, i.e., its `label` and `URL` attribute.

The `condition` and the `action` element may contain `communication-variable` elements. Their `name` attribute is used for specifying the variable's name. The `language` attribute defines the XML query language exploited for binding the variable. Communication variables are discussed in detail in Section 3.5.2.5.

The corresponding XML Schema definition which provides a formal specification of CAITL's syntax is illustrated in Figure 22:

```xml
<?xml version="1.0" encoding="utf-8" ?>
<xs:schema xmlns:xs="http://www.w3.org/2001/XMLSchema">
  <xs:element name="rule">
    <xs:complexType>
      <xs:sequence>
        <xs:element minOccurs="0" name="label" type="xs:string" />
        <xs:element minOccurs="0" name="description" type="xs:string" />
        <xs:element minOccurs="0" name="event">
          <xs:complexType>
            <xs:sequence>
              <xs:element name="subscription">
                <xs:complexType>
                  <xs:sequence>
                    <xs:element name="subscriptionstatement" type="xs:string" />
                  </xs:sequence>
                  <xs:attribute name="language" type="xs:string" use="required" />
                </xs:complexType>
              </xs:element>
            </xs:sequence>
          </xs:complexType>
        </xs:element>
        <xs:element name="condition">
          <xs:complexType>
            <xs:sequence>
              <xs:element minOccurs="0" maxOccurs="unbounded" name="communication-variable">
                <xs:complexType>
                  <xs:simpleContent>
                    <xs:extension base="xs:string">
                      <xs:attribute name="name" type="xs:string" use="required" />
                      <xs:attribute name="language" type="xs:string" use="required" />
                    </xs:extension>
                  </xs:simpleContent>
                </xs:complexType>
              </xs:element>
              <xs:element name="query">
                <xs:complexType>
                  <xs:sequence>
                    <xs:element name="querystatement" type="xs:string" />
                  </xs:sequence>
                  <xs:attribute name="language" type="xs:string" use="required" />
                </xs:complexType>
              </xs:element>
            </xs:sequence>
          </xs:complexType>
        </xs:element>
        <xs:element name="action">
          <xs:complexType>
            <xs:sequence>
              <xs:element minOccurs="0" maxOccurs="unbounded" name="communication-variable">
                <xs:complexType>
                  <xs:simpleContent>
                    <xs:extension base="xs:string">
                      <xs:attribute name="name" type="xs:string" use="required" />
                      <xs:attribute name="language" type="xs:string" use="required" />
                    </xs:extension>
                  </xs:simpleContent>
                </xs:complexType>
              </xs:element>
              <xs:element minOccurs="0" maxOccurs="unbounded" name="recommendation">
                <xs:complexType>
                  <xs:sequence>
                    <xs:element name="recommendationstatement" type="xs:string" />
                  </xs:sequence>
                  <xs:attribute name="identifier" type="xs:string" use="optional" />
                  <xs:attribute name="language" type="xs:string" use="required" />
                </xs:complexType>
              </xs:element>
              <xs:element minOccurs="0" maxOccurs="unbounded" name="selection">
                <xs:complexType>
                  <xs:sequence>
                    <xs:element name="querystatement" type="xs:string" />
                  </xs:sequence>
                  <xs:attribute name="identifier" type="xs:string" use="optional" />
                  <xs:attribute name="language" type="xs:string" use="required" />
                </xs:complexType>
              </xs:element>
              <xs:element name="template">
                <xs:complexType>
                  <xs:attribute name="label" type="xs:string" use="optional" />
                  <xs:attribute name="url" type="xs:string" use="required" />
                </xs:complexType>
              </xs:element>
            </xs:sequence>
          </xs:complexType>
        </xs:element>
      </xs:sequence>
      <xs:attribute name="id" type="xs:string" use="required" />
    </xs:complexType>
  </xs:element>
</xs:schema>
```

Figure 22: CAITL Syntax – XML Schema Definition

3.5.2.5 CAITL: Communication and Built-In Variables

CAITL's framework concept supports arbitrary component languages. This language heterogeneity requires a convention specifying how the applied component languages may communicate among each other. Hence, the framework has to provide a mechanism supporting the information exchange between the individual rule parts.

An example of such an information exchange drawing on the interaction between the rule's event and the corresponding condition part is the restriction of potential messages receivers to those located at a certain location (e.g. the selection of all users currently staying in a region where a blizzard warning was published). Such a restriction is specified within the rule's condition part employing the corresponding query language. However, the required location information (i.e., the region where the blizzard will occur) is provided by the *Event Service*, i.e., by the *Context Provider* component (cf. Section 3.5.1.7). In this case the location information is available in the rule's event part only and has to be communicated down to the rule's condition part.

The information exchange between the event, condition, and action part as well as the embedding of internal execution information is realized by means of variables. CAITL distinguishes between two types of variables, namely *communication* and *built-in variables* which are discussed subsequently:

Communication Variables

As described above, each of the rule parts may be specified employing different component languages. This language heterogeneity leads to different evaluation result "types" such as functional results (e.g. results of query languages such XPath) or bound variables (e.g. results of query languages based on the logical style such as F-Logic). Communication variables act as placeholders for these arbitrary values[15], hence, enabling to bind the results of the evaluation of a rule's event and condition part to the appropriate communication variables. The variables are communicated down to the condition and action part acting as restriction and/or configuration variable, i.e., they enable the exchange of results between the individual rule parts. Restriction variables narrow the results of the corresponding query statements using the variable's value(s) as restriction value (similar to the relational algebra's *restriction* operator). Configuration variables serve as an input for configuration languages such as the one applied to configure the underlying recommender system (cf. Section 4.2).

---

[15] Communication variables may be compared to logical variables known from logic programming (cf. Mitchell, 2003)

The following information chunks are exchanged between the rule parts (i.e., between the applied component languages) during rule execution:

- information about the triggering primitive or composite event
- information about the user

The binding of the communication variables is a two-tiered process. First, the results available after evaluating the appropriate component language statements (i.e., the results returned by the corresponding language processor, cf. *Event* and *Condition Handler* described in Section 3.5.1.2) are automatically bound to a corresponding XML based representation structure. Second, the desired values are extracted and bound to the appropriate communication variables (this binding process is exemplified at the end of this section).

Subsequently, appropriate XML based representations[16] are proposed:

- *event evaluation result*: The rule's event part expresses its interest in specific event(s) through a subscription statement compliant to the applied subscription language (cf. Section 2.3.4). The result of the evaluation of such an expression is an appropriate representation of the corresponding notification (in case of a primitive event subscription) or the sequence of notifications (in case of a composite event subscription). In addition to such event specific data the result may contain additional metadata such as a timestamp indicating the event's occurrence time[17] or the interval indicating the temporal parameter's value (in case of a composite event formed by a temporal conjunction operator, cf. Section 2.3.4). This result is bound to the internal XML event representation structure which is sketched in Figure 23:

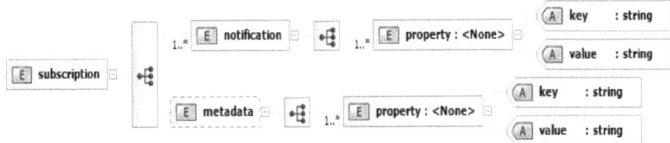

Figure 23: Communication Variables – Event Representation Format

The representation of the result is realized by one ore more `notification` elements. Each notification (i.e., the representation of a primitive event) is represented by a set of properties. These properties are represented by `property` elements including an

---

[16] It is worth noting that the proposed format is not unalterable and may be modified and extended by the language designer of a specific CAITL instance
[17] The definition of a composite event's timestamp depends on the underlying subscription language, i.e., on the semantics of the applied event algebra (cf. Section 2.3.4)

3.5 Conceptual Framework

appropriate `key` and `value` attribute. An example illustrating the bound result of an evaluation of a subscription to a primitive event is shown in Figure 24:

```xml
<?xml version="1.0" encoding="utf-8"?>
<subscription>
   <notification>
      <property key="region" value="Innsbruck" />
      <property key="weatherCode" value="BLIZ_TY_346020" />
      <property key="weatherLabel" value="Blizzard" />
      <property key="occurrenceTime" value="11:03:00" />
   </notification>
   <metadata>
      <property key="detection" value="2008-01-22 08:07:32" />
   </metadata>
</subscription>
```

Figure 24: Representation of a Blizzard Subscription

This example shows the binding of the event representation structure to the result of the evaluation of a rule's event part. As described above, the result of an evaluation of a subscription statement is a representation of the detected event. In the example above a "blizzard warning" event was detected and an appropriate notification was sent to the *Event Handler* (cf. Section 3.5.1.2) which in turn has bound the notification to the event representation format. The corresponding XML Schema definition is shown in Figure 25:

```xml
<?xml version="1.0" encoding="utf-8" ?>
<xs:schema xmlns:xs="http://www.w3.org/2001/XMLSchema">
   <xs:element name="subscription">
      <xs:complexType>
         <xs:sequence>
            <xs:element maxOccurs="unbounded" name="notification">
               <xs:complexType>
                  <xs:sequence>
                     <xs:element maxOccurs="unbounded" name="property">
                        <xs:complexType>
                           <xs:attribute name="key" type="xs:string" use="required" />
                           <xs:attribute name="value" type="xs:string" use="required" />
                        </xs:complexType>
                     </xs:element>
                  </xs:sequence>
               </xs:complexType>
            </xs:element>
            <xs:element minOccurs="0" name="metadata">
               <xs:complexType>
                  <xs:sequence>
                     <xs:element maxOccurs="unbounded" name="property">
                        <xs:complexType>
                           <xs:attribute name="key" type="xs:string" use="required" />
                           <xs:attribute name="value" type="xs:string" use="required" />
                        </xs:complexType>
                     </xs:element>
                  </xs:sequence>
               </xs:complexType>
            </xs:element>
         </xs:sequence>
      </xs:complexType>
   </xs:element>
</xs:schema>
```

Figure 25: Event Representation Structure– XML Schema Definition

- *condition evaluation result*: The rule's condition part determines the number of potential message receivers. The result of the condition evaluation is a set of users meeting the constraints specified in the corresponding query language. This result is bound to the internal XML user representation structure which is sketched in Figure 26:

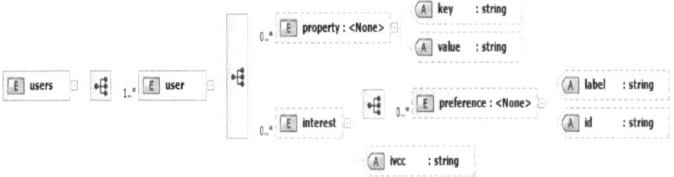

Figure 26: Communication Variables – User Representation Format

The representation of the result is realized by one ore more `user` elements. Each `user` element contains a sequence of `property` and `interest` elements. The former represents relevant (contextual) user information such as the user's current location, the master data, or the demographic data (see also Section 4.1). The latter represents the user's preferences concerning particular *Information Value chain Instances* such as events or sights. An example illustrating the bound result of an evaluation of a condition statement is shown in Figure 27:

```
<?xml version="1.0" encoding="utf-8"?>
<users>
    <user>
        <property key="firstName" value="Thomas" />
        <property key="lastName" value="Beer" />
        <property key="receivedSights" value="sight_20080926" />
        <property key="receivedSights" value="sight_19791205" />
        <interest ivcc="Events">
            <preference label="Entertainment" id="EV_ENT_0456" />
            <preference label="Sport" id="EV_SPO_0567" />
            <preference label="Heuriger / Burschenschenke" id="EV_HEU_9356" />
            <preference label="Music Events" id="EV_MUS_8245" />
            <preference label="Culinary Delights" id="EV_CUL_7134" />
        </interest>
        <interest ivcc="Sights">
            <preference label="Museums and Galleries" id="SI_ANG_5023" />
            <preference label="Experiencing Nature" id="SI_EXP_6023" />
        </interest>
    </user>
</users>
```

Figure 27: Representation of a User Binding

This example illustrates that the user "Thomas Beer" is interested in five types of events (*Entertainment*, *Sport*, *Heuriger / Burschenschenke*, *Music*, and *Culinary Delights*) and in sights related to *Experiencing Nature* (see also Section 4.4.2.1). The corresponding XML Schema definition is shown in Figure 28:

3.5 Conceptual Framework

```
<?xml version="1.0" encoding="utf-8" ?>
<xs:schema xmlns:xs="http://www.w3.org/2001/XMLSchema">
  <xs:element name="users">
    <xs:complexType>
      <xs:sequence>
        <xs:element minOccurs="1" maxOccurs="unbounded" name="user">
          <xs:complexType>
            <xs:sequence>
              <xs:element minOccurs="0" maxOccurs="unbounded" name="property">
                <xs:complexType>
                  <xs:attribute name="key" type="xs:string" use="optional" />
                  <xs:attribute name="value" type="xs:string" use="optional" />
                </xs:complexType>
              </xs:element>
              <xs:element minOccurs="0" maxOccurs="unbounded" name="interest">
                <xs:complexType>
                  <xs:sequence>
                    <xs:element minOccurs="0" maxOccurs="unbounded" name="preference">
                      <xs:complexType>
                        <xs:attribute name="label" type="xs:string" use="optional" />
                        <xs:attribute name="id" type="xs:string" use="optional" />
                      </xs:complexType>
                    </xs:element>
                  </xs:sequence>
                  <xs:attribute name="ivcc" type="xs:string" use="optional" />
                </xs:complexType>
              </xs:element>
            </xs:sequence>
          </xs:complexType>
        </xs:element>
      </xs:sequence>
    </xs:complexType>
  </xs:element>
</xs:schema>
```

Figure 28: User Representation Structure – XML Schema Definition

As described in Section 3.5.1.2, the *Event* and *Condition handler* components transform and automatically bind the results returned by the corresponding language processors to these representation structures. Having bound these results, particular result fragments can be extracted and bound to corresponding communication variables which may be applied as restriction and/or configuration variables afterwards.

Accessing particular result fragments is a three-tiered process drawing on XML query languages such as XPath (W3C, 1999) or XQuery (W3C, 2007):

1) Definition of communication variables using the `communication-variable` element[18]:

   ```
   <communication-variable name="v-name" />
   ```

2) Binding of the communication variable to the corresponding single- or multi-valued result fragment using an appropriate XML query language:

   ```
   < communication-variable name="v-name">
      <![CDATA[ query statement ]]>
   < communication-variable>
   ```

---

[18] The scope of communication variables is the rule

3) Using the bound communication variable as restriction or configuration variable drawing on the according access syntax: {$v-name$}

Currently, the employment of a multi-valued result has to be handled either during the binding process (e.g., using XQuery for creating native component language statements by iterating over the multi-valued result) or at the component language level (e.g., CWA-CL described in Section 4.2). However, this process could be facilitated by incorporating built-in functions aiming to ease the handling of multi-valued fields within component languages.

Subsequently, this three-tiered process is exemplified by drawing on the already known "blizzard warning" example:

```
<condition>
    <communication-variable name="location" language="XPath">
        <![CDATA[/subscription/notification/property[@key="region"]/@value]]>
    </communication-variable>
    <query language="HQL_3.3.1">
        <querystatement>
            <![CDATA[
                select distinct u from User u
                where u.currentLocation = loc AND
                loc.region = '($location$)'
            ]]>
        </querystatement>
    </query>
</condition>
```

Figure 29: Communication Variable, Example

Figure 29 illustrates the application of the *location* communication variable as restriction variable. It is exploited to restrict the potential message receivers to those currently staying in the region specified by the value of the *location* variable.

Built-in Variables

The incorporation of internal information concerning the rule execution such as its execution time is realized through built-in variables. Hence, these variables carry internal data and are automatically bound by the rule engine before starting the evaluation. The variables to be implemented depend on the specific language instance. To access the built-in variables it is proposed to employ the same access syntax as above and additionally apply a naming convention. The naming convention, e.g., using the prefix "built-in" facilitates the distinction between communication and built-in variables and supports the implementation of a corresponding rule interpreter. An example illustrating how a built-in variable is accessed within a rule's action part is presented in Section 3.5.2.6.

3.5.2.6 CAITL: Rule Execution Example

Based on the already known "blizzard example" introduced in Section 3.5.2.5 this section describes the rule execution process focusing on the dataflow between the parts of a rule. The employed example draws on an example rule which specifies, that affected users should be informed about appropriate sights in the case of a blizzard warning. The rule's relevant XML fragments are introduced successively. The execution process is triggered by a "successful" event subscription, i.e., if the *Event Service* (cf. Section 3.5.1.6) has successfully matched the rule's subscription to a detected event. The potential occurrence of a blizzard was reported by the *Publisher* component (cf. Section 3.5.1.5) sending an appropriate notification (see Figure 30):

```xml
<?xml version="1.0" encoding="utf-8"?>
<notification timestamp="2008-01-22 08:07:32">
    <property key="region" value="Innsbruck" />
    <property key="weatherCode" value="BLIZ_TY_346020" />
    <property key="weatherLabel" value="Blizzard" />
    <property key="occurrenceTime" value="11:03:00" />
</notification>
```

Figure 30: Blizzard Notification

The corresponding subscription is expressed in the rule's event part using the key/value based subscription language "imobile_sl_1.3" (cf. Section 4.2). The rule's event part is illustrated in Figure 31:

```xml
<?xml version="1.0" encoding="utf-8"?>
<rule id="ex_2008_02_20_4354">
    <event>
        <subscription language="imobile_sl_1.3">
            <subscriptionstatement>
                <![CDATA[
                    <filter>
                        <restriction>
                            <key> region </key>
                            <value> Innsbruck </value>
                            <type> string </type>
                            <operator> eq </operator>
                        </restriction>
                    </filter>
                ]]>
            </subscriptionstatement>
        </subscription>
    </event>
    .
    .
    .
</rule>
```

Figure 31: Blizzard Rule – Event Part

As discussed in Section 3.5.2.5, the result of a successful subscription contains the constituting event(s), i.e., the associated notification(s). The *Event Handler* (cf. Section 3.5.1.2) transforms the result and binds it to the appropriate representation structure (cf. Section 3.5.2.5) which is illustrated in Figure 32:

```xml
<?xml version="1.0" encoding="utf-8"?>
<subscription>
    <notification>
        <property key="region" value="Innsbruck" />
        <property key="weatherCode" value="BLIZ_TY_346020" />
        <property key="weatherLabel" value="Blizzard" />
        <property key="occurrenceTime" value="11:03:00" />
    </notification>
    <metadata>
        <property key="detection" value="2008-01-22 08:07:32" />
    </metadata>
</subscription>
```

Figure 32: Blizzard Rule – Subscription Representation

After completing the evaluation of the rule's event part the sequence control is passed to the *Condition Handler* (cf. Section 3.5.1.2) which is responsible for evaluating the rule's condition part. The condition specification is illustrated in Figure 33:

```xml
<?xml version="1.0" encoding="utf-8"?>
<rule id="ex_2008_02_20_4354">
    .
    .
    .
    <condition>
        <communication-variable name="location" language="XPath">
            <![CDATA[/subscription/notification/property[@key="region"]/@value]]>
        </communication-variable>
        <query language="HQL_3.3.1">
            <querystatement>
                <![CDATA[
                    select distinct u from User u
                    where u.currentLocation = loc AND
                    loc.region = '{$location$}'
                ]]>
            </querystatement>
        </query>
    </condition>
    .
    .
    .
</rule>
```

Figure 33: Blizzard Rule – Condition Part

The condition is evaluated to true if one or more users are currently staying in the region of Innsbruck. The example shows the application of the location communication-variable as restriction variable. The value to be bound to the "location" variable is extracted from the subscription representation (cf. Figure 32) exploiting an XPath expression. The *Condition Handler* applies this expression to the subscription representation and binds the result to the "location" variable. Afterwards, it replaces all occurrences of the "location" variable within the condition part with the corresponding value. After preprocessing, the native query statement (here, the Hibernate Query Language (HQL), cf. Hibernate, 2007 is employed) is passed to the related language processor. The result of this query is transformed and bound to the appropriate representation format (cf. Section 3.5.2.5). The corresponding representation is illustrated in Figure 34:

```xml
<?xml version="1.0" encoding="utf-8"?>
<users>
    <user>
        <property key="firstName" value="Thomas" />
        <property key="lastName" value="Beer" />
        <property key="receivedSights" value="sight_20080926" />
        <property key="receivedSights" value="sight_19791205" />
        <interest ivcc="Events">
            <preference label="Entertainment" id="EV_ENT_0456" />
            <preference label="Sport" id="EV_SPO_0567" />
            <preference label="Heuriger / Burschenschenke" id="EV_HEU_9356" />
            <preference label="Music Events" id="EV_MUS_8245" />
            <preference label="Culinary Delights" id="EV_CUL_7134" />
        </interest>
        <interest ivcc="Sights">
            <preference label="Museums and Galleries" id="SI_ANG_5023" />
            <preference label="Experiencing Nature" id="SI_EXP_6023" />
        </interest>
    </user>
</users>
```

Figure 34: Blizzard Rule – User Representation

Here, only one user fulfills the contextual restrictions posed by the query. After completing the evaluation of the rule's condition part the sequence control is passed to the *Action Handler* (cf. Section 3.5.1.2) which is responsible for executing the rule's action part. The corresponding XML fragment is illustrated in Figure 35:

```xml
<?xml version="1.0" encoding="utf-8"?>
<rule id="ex_2008_02_20_4354">
   .
   .
   .
   <action>
      <communication-variable name="preferences" language="XPath">
         <![CDATA[/users/user/interest[@ivcc="Sights"]]>
      </communication-variable>
      <communication-variable name="received_sights" language="XPath">
         <![CDATA[/user/property[@key="receivedSights"]]>
      </communication-variable>
      <recommendation identifier="sight" language="cwa_cl_0.9">
         <recommendationstatement>
            <![CDATA[
               <cwa_configuration>
                  <ivcc> Sight </ivcc>
                  <customerproperty>
                     <key>openingTimes</key>
                     <value>{$built-in.RuleExecutionDate$}</value>
                  </customerproperty>
                  <customerproperty>
                     <key>knd_received_sights</key>
                     <value>{$received_sights$}</value>
                  </customerproperty>
                  <customerproperty>
                     <key>classification</key>
                     <value>{$preferences$}</value>
                  </customerproperty>
                  <customerproperty>
                     <key>suitability</key>
                     <value>indoor</value>
                  </customerproperty>
               </cwa_configuration>
            ]]>
         </recommendationstatement>
      </recommendation>
      <template label="BlizzardWarning" url="./templates/"/>
   </action>
</rule>
```

Figure 35: Blizzard Rule – Action Part

As described in Section 3.5.2.3, the action execution may be separated into three steps:

1) *Message Instance* creation

2) message rendering, i.e., creation of the *Final Message*

3) message sending

These three steps are executed for each of the previously retrieved users (i.e., for the users retrieved by executing the rule's condition part). The IVCIs contained in the *Message Instance* are retrieved exploiting the underlying recommender (here, a knowledge-based recommender). The recommender is configured exploiting the corresponding configuration language "cwa_cl_0.9" (cf. Section 4.2) drawing on the configuration variable "preferences". This variable is bound to the user's preferences regarding sights. The binding of the communication variables is summarized in Figure 36:

3.5 Conceptual Framework

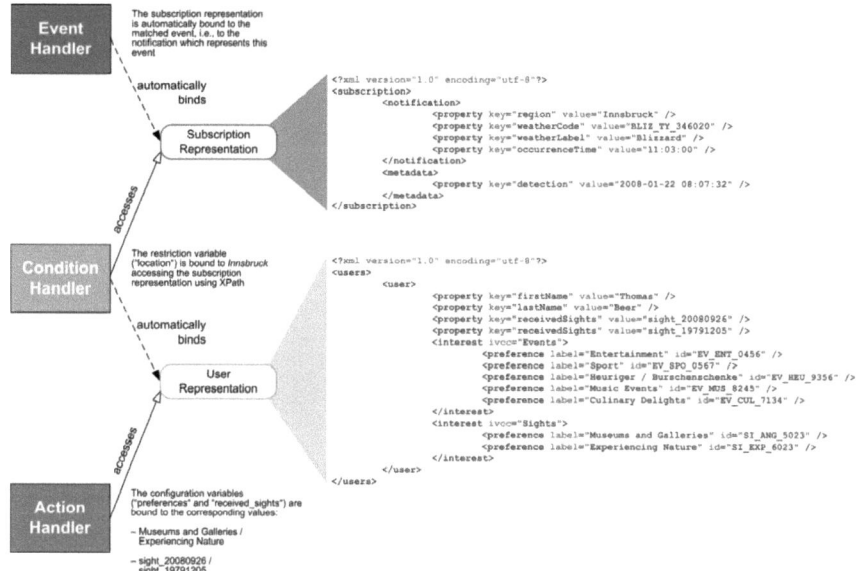

Figure 36: Binding of the Communication Variables

After creating the *Message Instance* the *Final Message* is generated exploiting the specified template (cf. Sections 3.5.1.9 and 4.3.2.1). Subsequently, the message is scheduled for delivery (cf. Sections 3.5.1.10 and 4.3.2.1).

4 Case Study: innsbruck.mobile

Everything comes too late for those who only wait

Elbert Hubbard (1856 - 1915)

innsbruck.mobile is a mobile tourist guide for the destination of Innsbruck supporting customers in all trip phases by providing relevant information such as attractions & sights, events, gastronomy and weather forecasts. It is based on the *etPlanner* framework (Höpken et al., 2006) supporting the flexible and rapid implementation of context-aware mobile tourist guides. *innsbruck.mobile* provides both *push* and *pull* based information services. The former, which is subsequently denoted as CAIPS-IM, was derived from the conceptual framework introduced in Section 3.5 and is discussed in detail subsequently[19]. This implementation acts as the basis for a qualitative evaluation of the requirements posed by CAIPS (cf. Sections 4.4 and 3.3 respectively). The relationship between the conceptual framework of CAIPS, the etPlanner framework, CAIPS-IM, and *innsbruck.mobile* is illustrated in Figure 37:

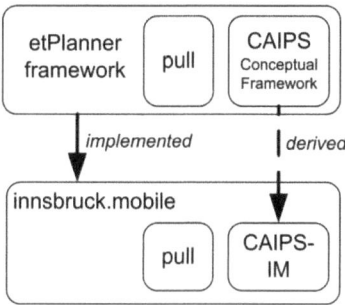

Figure 37: Relating CAIPS, CAIPS-IM, etPlanner, and innsbruck.mobile

As described in Section 3.5, the conceptual framework is fundamentally composed of a *reference model* and a *rule language framework*. The former facilitates the design of a specific

---

[19] For details concerning the pull part of *innsbruck.mobile* it is referred to Beer et. al (2008)

context-aware information push system by specifying its fundamental functional and logical parts. Consequently, the architecture of CAIPS-IM was derived from this reference model. The architecture as well as the respective counterparts of the reference model are described in Section 4.3. The latter provides a language framework facilitating the development of the corresponding rule language. As described in Section 3.5.2, this language framework supports the development of specific CAITL instances exploiting arbitrary component languages. The rule language applied in CAIPS-IM (i.e., CAITL-IM) as well as the involved component languages, namely "imobile_sl", "Hibernate Query Language", and "CWA-CL" are introduced in Section 4.2.

However, before describing the underlying architecture and the corresponding rule language, context representation related issues of CAIPS-IM are discussed in Section 4.1.

4.1 CAIPS-IM: Context Representation

As described in Section 3.5.2.3, within CAITL, the condition is expressed as a truth valued query which is interpreted as a truth value if the query's result is non empty. The query restricts the potential message receivers by posing restrictions upon the corresponding context repository. A main advantage of CAIPS is its support of arbitrary context repositories, i.e., the independence from specific representation techniques (cf. Sections 3.5.2.2 and 3.5.2.3). This section describes the relevant contextual information categories and their conceptual representation as employed within CAIPS-IM.

To support the user-centric approach of CAIPS (cf. Sections 3.5.1.1 and 3.5.2.3) contextual information is represented in a user-centric style as well (see Figure 38):

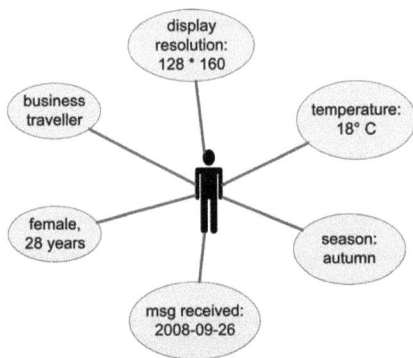

Figure 38: User-Centric Context Representation

As discussed in Section 2.2.1, the relevant context categories may vary from application to application. The aim of building categories is to identify the contextual information pieces most relevant for the corresponding application. The context categories particularly relevant for

4.1 CAIPS-IM: Context Representation

CAIPS-IM are discussed subsequently. Based on the categorizations from Beer et al. (2007), Chen & Kotz (2000), Dey & Abowd (2000b), and Schmidt et al. (1999) the following context categories were identified:

- *User*: This category represents relevant user information such as demographic and master data
- *Environment*: This category represents information regarding the user's environment such as the current weather at the user's current location
- *Time*: This category represents temporal information such as the current time or the current travel season
- *Computing*: This category represents information regarding the user's mobile device such as the devices' display resolution
- *Travel*: This category represents travel specific information such as the specification of the travel category, i.e., whether the user is on a business trip or on holidays
- *Message*: This category represents information regarding the *Final Messages* a user has already received such as contained IVCIs (cf. Section 3.4.3) or the timestamp when the *Final Message* was received

The context categories and corresponding examples relevant for CAIPS-IM are summarized in Table 7:

Context Category	*Example*
User	the user's demographic data
Environment	current weather
Time	time of the day, time of the year
Computing	employed mobile device, display resolution
Travel	business travel, family travel
Message	received message instances

Table 7: Context Categories as Employed in CAIPS-IM

Based on these categorizations, i.e., after identifying the relevant contextual information pieces, the *conceptual schema*[20] was created. It provides a high-level description of the

---

[20] Usually, the architecture of database systems is divided into three or four levels namely, external, conceptual, logical, and internal. The logical level (which is also known as *implementation conceptual level*) is often not explicitly mentioned (Date, 2004; Elmasri & Navathe, 2006; Halpin, 2001).

corresponding structure of the underlying database (cf. Section 4.3.2.1). The conceptual schema represents the contextual information based on:

- concepts (i.e., types of objects, or entities; see also Section 3.4.2)
- relationships between these concepts
- roles these concepts may play
- structural constraints such as cardinalities

The conceptual schema representing the contextual information as applied in CAIPS-IM is illustrated in the UML class diagram below (see Figure 39):

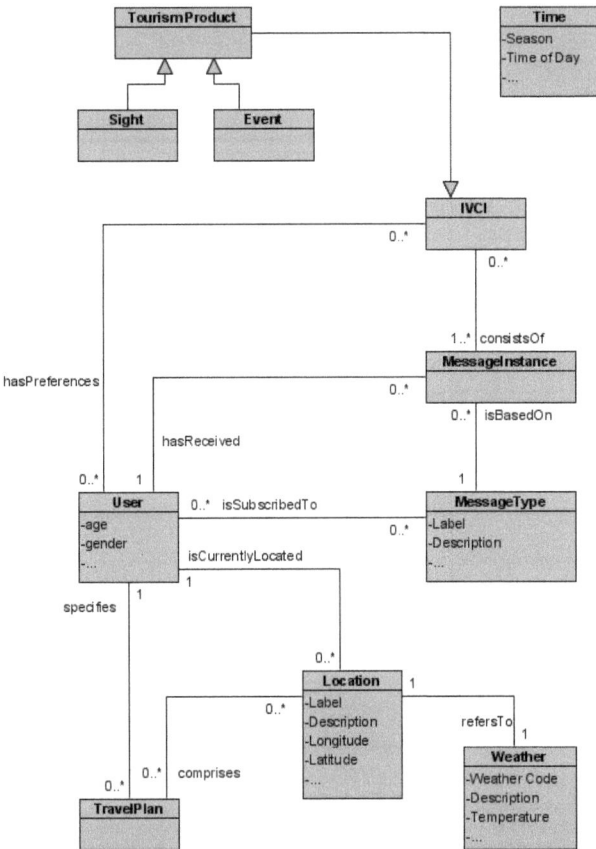

Figure 39: Contextual Information, Conceptual Representation

The contextual information regarding the *computing* category is not stored in the underlying database as it is determined at runtime employing *WURFL*[21] and is only relevant for the *pull* part of *innsbruck.mobile*.

Details concerning the implementation of the conceptual schema are discussed in Section 4.3.2.1.

4.2 CAIPS-IM: CAITL-IM

This section introduces CAITL-IM, the context-aware information triggering language applied in CAIPS-IM. Moreover, two of the rules applied in CAIPS-IM are presented (cf. Section 4.2.1).

CAITL-IM was derived and specified based on the modular language framework introduced in Section 3.5.2. This framework supports the development of specific CAITL instances exploiting arbitrary component languages. Subsequently, the component languages applied in CAITL-IM are described:

CAITL-IM – event part: imobile_sl

As explained in Section 3.5.2.3, CAITL's event part is specified using a subscription language. CAITL-IM employs the proprietary filter language "imobile_sl" which is based on the content-based filter model (cf. Section 2.3.2.3). It applies key/value pairs and appropriate comparison operators to specify the corresponding subscription statement. A filter may be composed of one or more restrictions with respect to the properties of the notifications to be filtered. These restrictions may be compared to the "where" clause of an SQL statement; however, in "imobile_sl" the contributing restrictions are combined using a logical conjunction exclusively.

The XML based syntax of "imobile_sl" is illustrated in Figure 40 using an XML Schema definition:

---

[21] WURFL is a device description repository, i.e., a catalogue of mobile device information and a framework supporting the implementation of adaptive mobile applications (Passani, 2008)

```xml
<?xml version="1.0" encoding="utf-8" ?>
<xs:schema xmlns:xs="http://www.w3.org/2001/XMLSchema">
  <xs:element name="filter">
    <xs:complexType>
      <xs:sequence>
        <xs:element maxOccurs="unbounded" name="restriction">
          <xs:complexType>
            <xs:sequence>
              <xs:element name="key" type="xs:string" />
              <xs:element name="value" type="xs:string" />
              <xs:element name="type" type="xs:string" />
              <xs:element name="operator">
                <xs:simpleType>
                  <xs:restriction base="xs:string">
                    <xs:enumeration value="lt" />
                    <xs:enumeration value="gt" />
                    <xs:enumeration value="eq" />
                    <xs:enumeration value="neq" />
                  </xs:restriction>
                </xs:simpleType>
              </xs:element>
            </xs:sequence>
          </xs:complexType>
        </xs:element>
      </xs:sequence>
    </xs:complexType>
  </xs:element>
</xs:schema>
```

Figure 40: XML Schema imobile sl 1.3

The filter's root element contains one or more `restriction` elements. Each restriction element is composed of a `key`, `value`, `operator`, and `type` element. The former three elements are exploited for specifying restrictions regarding the value(s) of a notification's properties. The `type` element is exploited to facilitate the implementation of the underlying filter engine. For example, to filter all notifications whose region property's value is equal to "Innsbruck" the following "imobile_sl" syntax is applied (see Figure 41):

```xml
<filter>
    <restriction>
        <key> region </key>
        <value> Innsbruck </value>
        <type> string </type>
        <operator> eq </operator>
    </restriction>
</filter>
```

Figure 41: Example imobile_sl

CAITL-IM – Condition Part

As discussed in Section 3.5.2.3, CAITL's condition part is specified exploiting query languages. CAITL-IM employs the object-oriented "Hibernate Query Language" (Hibernate, 2007) for specifying appropriate user-centric queries.

CAITL-IM – Action Part: CWA-CL

As described in Section 3.5.2.2, a rule's action part is specified exploiting specific recommender languages as well as standard query languages. CAITL-IM employs "CWA-CL" for specifying the recommender specific section of the corresponding action part. "CWA-CL" is a proprietary language enabling to "configure" the underlying knowledge-based recommender (CWA, cf. Section 4.3.1.1), i.e., to bind the required user properties to the appropriate values. Which user properties have to be bound depends on the employed filters (cf. Section 4.3.1.1). The result of the evaluation of such an IVCC-centric configuration statement is a set of ranked IVCIs which are well suited for the user in question. IVCC-centric means that a specific configuration has to be specified for each IVCC to be recommended. This goes along with the functionality of the applied knowledge-based recommender which is based on a number of IVCC related filter rules (cf. Section 4.3.1.1).

The corresponding XML Schema definition is illustrated in Figure 42:

```xml
<?xml version="1.0" encoding="utf-8" ?>
<xs:schema xmlns:xs="http://www.w3.org/2001/XMLSchema">
  <xs:element name="cwa_configuration">
    <xs:complexType>
      <xs:sequence>
        <xs:element name="ivcc" type="xs:string" />
        <xs:element maxOccurs="unbounded" name="customerproperty">
          <xs:complexType>
            <xs:sequence>
              <xs:element name="key" type="xs:string" />
              <xs:element name="value" type="xs:string" />
            </xs:sequence>
          </xs:complexType>
        </xs:element>
      </xs:sequence>
    </xs:complexType>
  </xs:element>
</xs:schema>
```

Figure 42: XML Schema – CWA-CL

As described above, a configuration of the underlying knowledge-based recommender is IVCC-centric. The corresponding IVCC is specified using the `ivcc` element. The required user properties are bound exploiting the `customerproperty` element which is composed of a `key` and a `value` element. The former denotes the name of the user property as applied in the corresponding filter rule. The latter specifies the value(s) to be bound.

The example in Figure 43 illustrates the binding of the user properties employed in the associated filter rules which are used for suggesting appropriate sights:

```xml
<?xml version="1.0" encoding="utf-8"?>
<cwa_configuration>
    <ivcc> Sight </ivcc>
    <customerproperty>
        <key>knd_received_sights</key>
        <value>{$received_sights$}</value>
    </customerproperty>
    <customerproperty>
        <key>classification</key>
        <value>{$preferences$}</value>
    </customerproperty>
    <customerproperty>
        <key>suitability</key>
        <value>indoor</value>
    </customerproperty>
</cwa_configuration>
```

Figure 43: CWA-CL Example

The applied filter rules constrain the available sights by posing restrictions concerning the user's preferences, the already received sights, and whether the potential sight is located indoor.

4.2.1 CAITL-IM: Applied Message Types & Corresponding Rules

This section introduces two of the rules applied in CAIPS-IM. They were employed for creating two of the *Message Types* introduced in Section 1.1.2, namely:

- *Good Morning Message*: Messages of this type provide the tourists with information regarding suitable sights and the current weather (see also Section 1.1.2).
- *Event Notification*: Messages of this type inform the tourists about events they might be interested in and which will take place within the next few days (see also Section 1.1.2).

Both rules are subscribed for internal events (cf. Section 3.5.1.5). This is shown by the corresponding subscription statement which exploits cron-expressions (OpenSymphony, 2008a) for expressing the related subscription. The corresponding *EventGenerator* (cf. Section 4.3.2.1) is implemented based on the Quartz job scheduling API (OpenSymphony, 2008b). The appropriate CAITL-IM rules are presented below:

4.2 CAIPS-IM: CAITL-IM   99
Good Morning Message Type:

```xml
<?xml version="1.0" encoding="utf-8"?>
<rule id="gmp_156239831790714432">
    <label><![CDATA[GoodMorningMessage]]></label>
    <event>
        <subscription language="imobile_sl_1.3">
            <subscriptionstatement><![CDATA[
                <filter>
                    <restriction>
                        <key> cron </key>
                        <value> 20 45 07 08 2008 </value>
                        <type> string </type>
                        <operator> eq </operator>
                    </restriction>
                </filter>]]>
            </subscriptionstatement>
        </subscription>
    </event>
    <condition>
        <query language="HQL_3.3.1">
            <querystatement><![CDATA[
                select distinct u from HibUser as u, HibSubscription as sub,
                HibPushMessage as pm, HibTranslationAttribute as ta,
                HibTranslation as trans, HibLanguage as lang
                where sub.user = u AND sub.pushMessage = pm AND
                ta = pm.label AND
                pm.active = true AND
                sub.isActive = true AND
                trans.value='Good Morning Message'
                AND trans.Language = lang AND lang.value = 'en_GB' AND
                trans.TranslationAttribute = ta ]]>
            </querystatement>
        </query>
    </condition>
    <action>
        <communication-variable name="preferences" language="XPath">
            <![CDATA[/users/user/interest[@ivcc="Sights"]]]>
        </communication-variable>
        <communication-variable name="received_sights" language="XPath">
            <![CDATA[/user/property[$key="receivedSights"]]]>
        </communication-variable>
        <recommendation identifier="sight" language="cwa_cl_0.9">
            <recommendationstatement><![CDATA[
                <cwa_configuration>
                    <ivcc> Sight </ivcc>
                    <customerproperty>
                        <key>openingTimes</key>
                        <value>{$built-in.RuleExecutionDate$}</value>
                    </customerproperty>
                    <customerproperty>
                        <key>knd_received_sights</key>
                        <value>{$receivedSights$}</value>
                    </customerproperty>
                    <customerproperty>
                        <key>classification</key>
                        <value>{$preferences$}</value>
                    </customerproperty>
                </cwa_configuration> ]]>
            </recommendationstatement>
        </recommendation>
        <selection identifier="CityWeather" language="HQL_3.3.1">
            <querystatement>
                <![CDATA[
                select w from CityWeather w, City c where w.city = c AND
                w.forecastDate = {$built-in.RuleExecutionDate$} ]]>
            </querystatement>
        </selection>
        <template label="GoodMorningMessage" url="./templates/" />
    </action>
</rule>
```

Event Notification Message Type:

```xml
<?xml version="1.0" encoding="utf-8"?>
<rule id="en_476197480243217408">
  <label><![CDATA[EventNotification]]></label>
  <event>
    <subscription language="imobile_sl_1.3">
      <subscriptionstatement><![CDATA[
            <filter>
               <restriction>
                  <key> cron </key>
                  <value> 20 45 06 08 2008 </value>
                  <type> string </type>
                  <operator> eq </operator>
               </restriction>
            </filter>
      ]]></subscriptionstatement>
    </subscription>
  </event>
  <condition>
    <query language="HQL_3.3.1">
      <querystatement><![CDATA[
            select u from HibUser as u, HibSubscription as sub, HibPushMessage as           pm,
HibTranslationAttribute as ta, HibTranslation as trans,              HibLanguage as lang
            where sub.user = u AND sub.pushMessage = pm AND sub.isActive = true AND           ta
= pm.label AND pm.active = true AND trans.value='Event                     Notification' AND
trans.Language = lang AND lang.value = 'en_GB' AND
            trans.TranslationAttribute = ta]]>
      </querystatement>
    </query>
  </condition>
  <action>
    <communication-variable name="preferences" language="XPath">
      <![CDATA[/users/user/interest[@ivcc="Events"]]]>
    </communication-variable>
    <communication-variable name="received_events" language="XPath">
      <![CDATA[/user/property[@key="receivedEvents"]]]>
    </communication-variable>
    <communication-variable name="sendingDistance" language="XPath">
      <![CDATA[/user/property[@key="en_sendingDistance"]]]>
    </communication-variable>
    <recommendation identifier="event" language="cwa_cl_0.9">
      <recommendationstatement><![CDATA[
         <cwa_configuration>
           <ivcc> Event </ivcc>
            <customerproperty>
             <key>startDate</key>
             <value>
              {built-in.Add({$built-in.RuleExecutionDate$};{$sendingDistance$})}
             </value>
            </customerproperty>
            <customerproperty>
             <key>endDate</key>
             <value>
              {built-in.Add({$built-in.RuleExecutionDate$};{$sendingDistance$})}
             </value>
            </customerproperty>
            <customerproperty>
             <key>knd_received_events</key>
             <value>{$received_events$}</value>
            </customerproperty>
            <customerproperty>
             <key>classification</key>
             <value>{$preferences$}</value>
            </customerproperty>
         </cwa_configuration>
      ]]></recommendationstatement>
    </recommendation>
    <template label="EventNotification" url="./templates/" />
  </action>
</rule>
```

4.3 CAIPS-IM: Architecture

This section presents the architecture of *innsbruck.mobile* focusing on its *push* component whose design was derived from the reference model introduced in Section 3.5.1. As proposed by

4.3 CAIPS-IM: Architecture

Clements et al. (2002) and Kruchten (1995), the architecture is described exploiting different *views*. The *system overview* is illustrated in Section 4.3.1. The fundamental components of CAIPS-IM are described in the *conceptual view* in Section 4.3.2. The *deployment view* illustrating the physical runtime environment is presented in Section 4.3.3.

4.3.1 innsbruck.mobile – System Overview

This section provides an overview about the constituting components of *innsbruck.mobile*. They are sketched in Figure 44 using a UML *composite structure diagram* (Ambler, 2004):

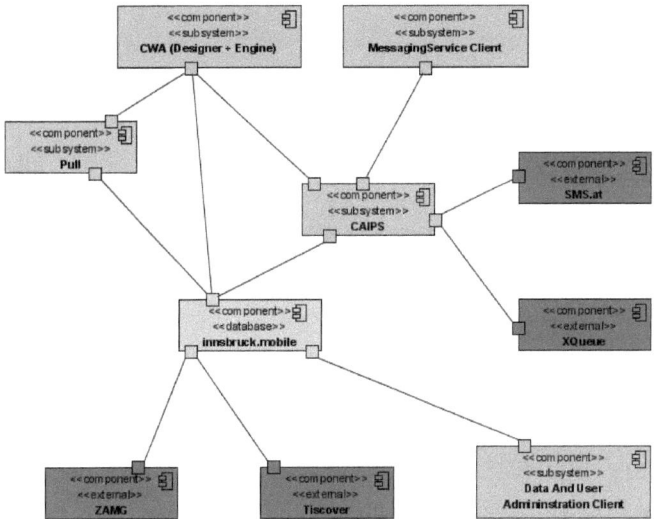

Figure 44: innsbruck.mobile System Overview

The system is built around a central relational database management system using PostgreSQL (PostgreSQL Global Development Group, 2008). The database (innsbruck.mobile database) stores both context and IVCI relevant data. Corresponding instance data is maintained by several components. Data access services from external systems such as *Tiscover* (tisCOVER, 2008) and *ZAMG* (ZAMG, 2008) are employed to provide the system with up to date information regarding tourism services and weather. These data access services may be compared to *Context Providers* and *IVCI Providers* as discussed in Section 3.5.1.7 and 3.5.1.11 respectively. Furthermore, authorized users may update, delete, or complete this data using the *Data and User Administration Client*. The fundamental components of *innsbruck.mobile*, namely its *push* and *pull* subsystems are implemented using web application technologies. The first, i.e., CAIPS-IM, exploits an external SMS as well as an external, managed e-mail gateway for realizing the message sending functionality, namely *SMS.at* (sms.at, 2008) and *XQueue* (XQueue

GmbH, 2008) respectively. The *Messaging Service Client* provides a high-level user interface to allow authorized service providers to create, edit, and delete CAITL rules. Both, CAIPS-IM and the pull subsystems exploit the *CWA* subsystem which is responsible for generating knowledge-based recommendations regarding tourism services. The *CWA* subsystem is described in more detail in Section 4.3.1.1.

4.3.1.1 CWA Subsystem

The recommender system employed within *innsbruck.mobile* was implemented based on the *Advisor Suite* framework (Jannach, 2004). This framework facilitates the development of conversational, knowledge-based recommender systems through graphical development tools and code templates. Hence, the framework significantly reduces development and maintenance costs.

Technically, the applied recommender application (i.e., the *CWA* subsystem) is built on Java & Java Servlet technologies and deployed in a standard servlet container (cf. Section 4.3.3). Therefore, it could be seamlessly integrated into the overall *innsbruck.mobile* architecture (Beer et al., 2008). In general, the *CWA* subsystem can be separated into two components, namely the *advisor designer* and the *advisor engine*. The former is, among other things, exploited for specifying filtering rules. The latter "evaluates" these rules at runtime and determines the appropriate IVCI(s) for each user.

The filter rules (also known as recommendation rules) define constraints relating user properties (e.g., preferences, the user's current situation) with IVCC properties (cf. user and product model in Section 2.4). These constraints are represented in the conditional style (cf. Section 2.1.2.2). The corresponding condition consists of an expression on arbitrary user properties specifying when this recommendation rule has to be applied. The rule's consequent specifies corresponding restrictions on the properties of the IVCCs. The screenshot in Figure 45 illustrates the definition of a filter rule which excludes the sights that a user has already received from the list of potential available sights:

4.3 CAIPS-IM: Architecture

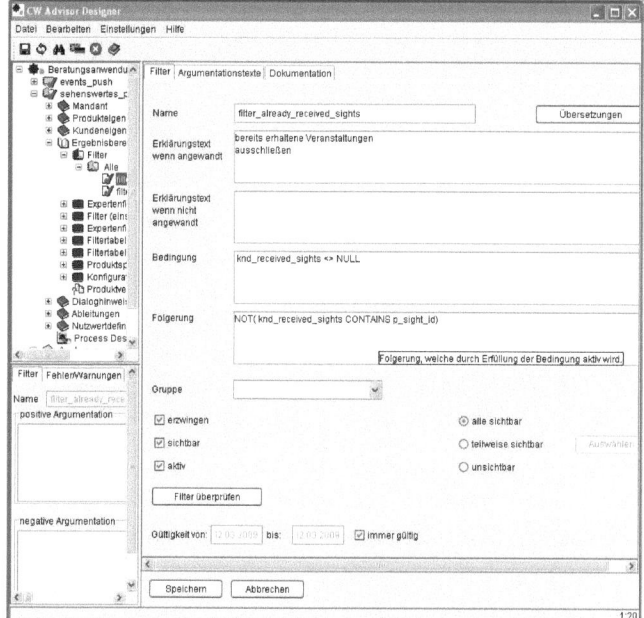

Figure 45: CWA – Specification of Recommendation Rules

The filter illustrated in the example above associates the user and the product model exploiting the user property "knd_received_sights" and the product property "p_sight_id". The user property is bound at runtime exploiting the corresponding configuration language (cf. Sections 3.5.2.6 and 4.2). Such a recommendation rule[22] may be exploited, for example, to avoid *Duplicate Messages* (cf. Section 3.4.7).

For each IVCC to be suggested a set of such filters may be specified. These filters are evaluated at runtime and serve to sort out IVCIs not favorable for the user. This recommendation functionality provided by the *advisor engine* can be exploited from external applications by means of an API or via web-service calls. Both interfaces are employed at rule execution time to bind the corresponding user properties and to consequently determine the appropriate IVCIs (cf. recommender component in Section 4.3.2.1).

For more details concerning the CW Advisor system it is referred to Jannach (2004) and Zanker & Jessenitschnig (2008).

---

[22] It is worth noting that the *advisor engine* evaluates these rules by a specific algorithm instead of exploiting a classical rule-engine. For details it is referred to Jannach (2006).

4.3.2 CAIPS-IM – Conceptual View

Inspired by the *design viewpoint* of Kruchten (Kruchten, 2003) this section discusses the structural and behavioral aspects of CAIPS as implemented within *innsbruck.mobile*. The conceptual view may also be considered as the combination of the *logical* and the *process* view as discussed in Kruchten (1995). The basic building blocks of CAIPS-IM are summarized in Figure 46:

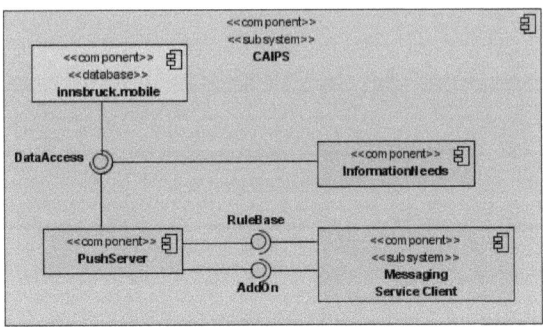

Figure 46: innsbruck.mobile – Basic Building Blocks of CAIPS-IM

The central building block is the *PushServer* component encapsulating the core functionalities for declaratively creating and sending tailored messages. It is discussed in detail in Section 4.3.2.1.

Both stakeholders, i.e., the service provider and the user are interacting with the *PushServer*. On the one hand the service provider interacts with the *PushServer* to create, update, and delete *Message Types* (i.e., CAITL-IM rules) as well as for invoking add-on functionalities such as to manually send messages. The corresponding user interfaces are implemented within the *MessagingServiceClient* component which is discussed in Section 4.3.2.2. On the other hand the user interacts with the *PushServer* to specify his information needs. The *InformationNeeds* component provides the user with a graphical interface to specify his preferences regarding *Information Value Chain Concepts*, to subscribe for *Message Types*, and to specify fundamental master data such as his name and his preferred language. This component is realized as part of the etPlanner's innovative self-adapting pull component (Höpken et al., 2008).

These two interfaces can be compared to the *User Interfaces* entity of the reference model introduced in Section 3.5.1.13.

4.3.2.1 PushServer

The *PushServer* provides the fundamental functionalities for declaratively creating and sending tailored messages. It is illustrated in Figure 47 using a composite-structure diagram

4.3 CAIPS-IM: Architecture

showing its internal structure, i.e., its fundamental components and ports (a port may be regarded as a further refined interface, cf. Ambler, 2004 and Gorton, 2006). These components are explained subsequently.

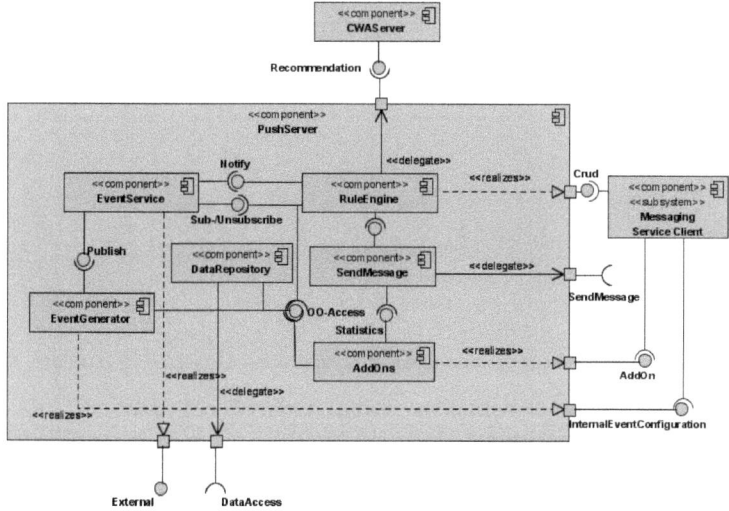

Figure 47: PushServer

DataRepository: Provides methods for accessing the underlying relational database (cf. innsbruck.mobile database in Section 4.3.1) in an implementation neutral way exploiting the object/relational mapping and query framework *Hibernate* (Hibernate, 2008). This component can be considered as an implementation of the reference model's *IVCI* and *Context Repository* as discussed in Section 3.5.1.1.

EventGenerator: Acts as a *producer* of internal events, i.e., reports occurrences caused by the system's internal behavior such as when a certain point of time is reached. This component mirrors the reference model's *Publisher* entity which is described in Section 3.5.1.5.

To facilitate adding new event generators, i.e., to support extensibility, the *creation* of internal event generators is realized employing the *Factory* pattern (Gamma et al., 1995). The *IEventGenerator* interface, i.e., its implementations represents the *type* of an internal *EventGenerator* such as a *TimeEventGenerator*. It acts as a kind of container for *real* implementations of an event generator, i.e., it controls the *EventGenratorInstances*. These provide the functionalities for observing system internal occurrences and for publishing the associated notifications. Using the Factory pattern significantly reduces the complexity of creating new *EventGenerators* further supporting etPlanner's framework concept. The internal structure is illustrated in Figure 48:

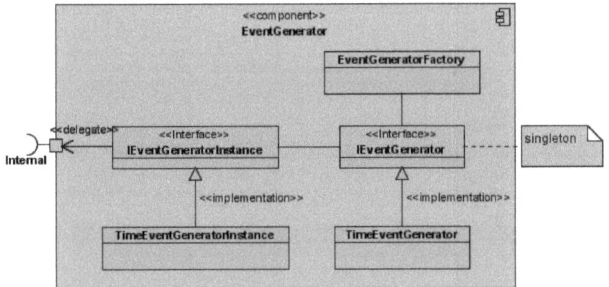

Figure 48: EventGenerator

Figure 49 illustrates the *EventGenerator* creation process using a UML sequence diagram:

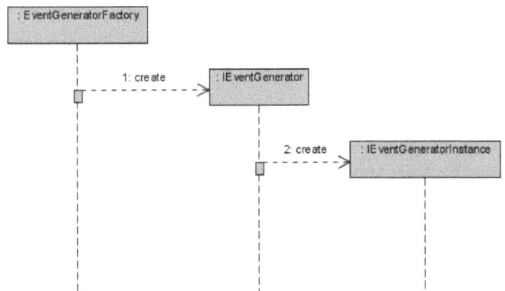

Figure 49: Creating an EventGenerator

EventService: Mediates between *EventGenerator* and *RuleEngine*, i.e., it tests notifications for matching subscriptions and forwards successfully matched notifications to the appropriate subscribers, i.e., to the *EventHandler*. This component corresponds to the *Event Service* entity introduced in Section 3.5.1.6.

SendMessage: This component provides the functionalities for sending the messages using the receiver's preferred communication channel. Currently, two communication channels are supported, namely SMS and e-mail. The service is realized by an internal gateway and its associated external gateway services, namely *XQueue* and *SMS.at*. The internal gateway acts as a central connector to the external gateways. It provides services for transforming a message into the required format and for routing the message to the appropriate external gateway. The

4.3 CAIPS-IM: Architecture

Message Gateway (cf. Section 3.5.1.10) represents the corresponding counterpart within the reference model.

***AddOns*:** This component implements value adding services as described in the reference model's *Add-On Services* entity. The following value adding services were implemented within CAIPS-IM:

- Manual sending of messages: Enables the sending of messages to a predefined set of users. For this, the service provider basically selects desired receivers from a list of available users and specifies (static) messages.
- Message tracing: This component offers required services for tracking sent messages. It provides methods for transforming the raw tracking data into a format that is appropriate to the service provider. In addition it implements services for searching specific messages such as selecting all messages sent within a given timeframe.
- Simulate Message Sending: This component provides methods to test the execution of new rules. A simulation results in a list of potential message receivers and the respective *Final Message(s)* (cf. Section 3.4.5).

***RuleEngine*:** The *RuleEngine* is responsible for interpreting the CAITL-IM rules (cf. Section 4.2). Its design is illustrated in Figure 50:

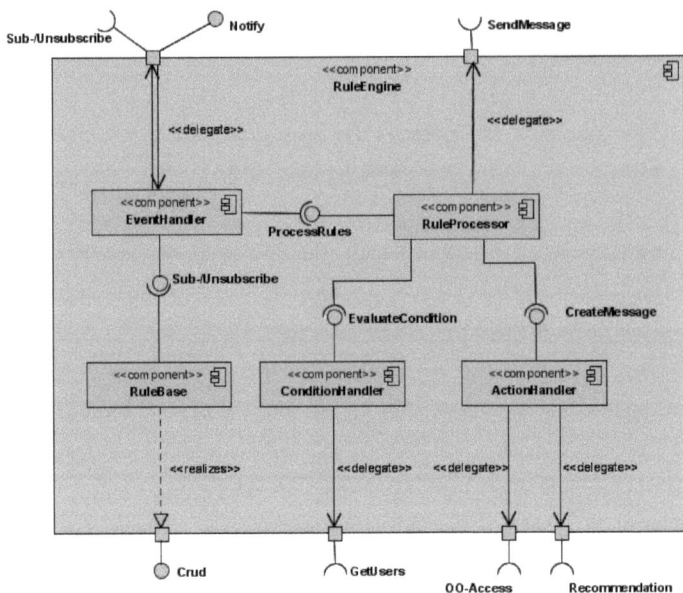

Figure 50: RuleEngine

The rule engine, which corresponds to the reference model's *Rule Interpreter* (cf. Section 3.5.1.2), is composed of five fundamental components:

- *EventHandler*: This encapsulates the functionalities for subscribing and unsubscribing. It determines the rule(s) associated with the incoming notification and passes these to the *RuleProcessor* for further processing.
- *RuleProcessor*: Coordinates the interaction of the involved components. Moreover it offers some utility functions such as the computation of a message's sending timestamp.
- *ConditionHandler*: Transforms the rule's condition definition (cf. Section 4.2) into the appropriate query language and delegates the query processing to the associated query engine. The *ConditionHandler* uses the object-oriented query language HQL (Hibernate, 2007) to access the object-oriented *DataRepository*. Subsequently, the query results comprising a number of potential message receivers are forwarded to the *ActionHandler* by the *RuleProcessor*.
- *ActionHandler*: Responsible for creating the *Message Instance* (cf. Section 3.4.4) and the corresponding *Final Message(s)* (see Section 3.4.5). Its internal structure is illustrated in Figure 51:

4.3 CAIPS-IM: Architecture

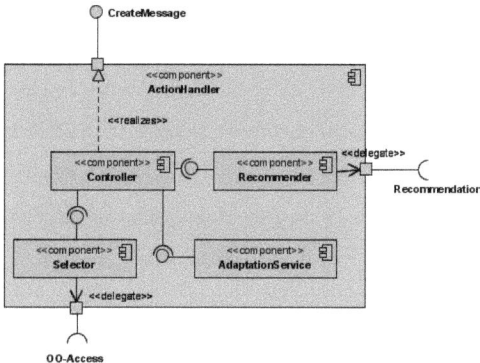

Figure 51: ActionHandler

The message creation process is realized in a two-tiered process (see Figure 52):

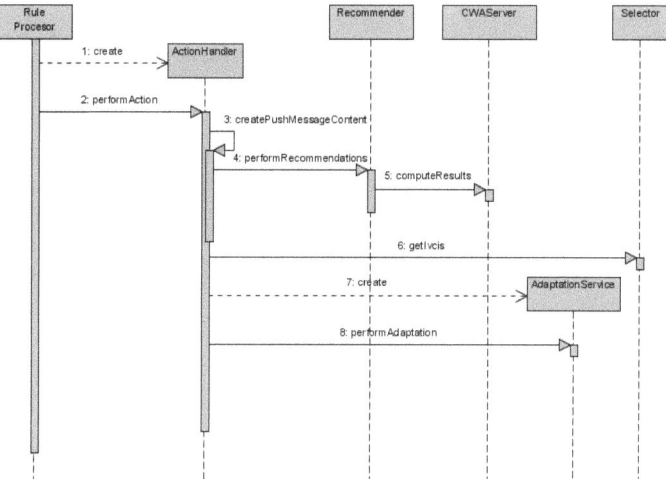

Figure 52: Message Creation Process

First, the *Message Instance* (cf. Section 3.4.4) is created exploiting the corresponding *Recommender* and/or *Selector* components. The former evaluates the rule's action part (cf. Section 4.2) exploiting the CWA subsystem (cf. Section 4.3.1.1). The latter evaluates the selection part of the rule's action component exploiting the underlying *DataRepository*. These two components correspond to the reference model's *IVCI Retriever* entity (cf. Section 3.5.1.3), i.e., to the *Recommender* and *IVCI Retrieval* entity respectively.

Second, the message is rendered according to the users preferred communication channel(s). The rendering process is encapsulated within the *AdaptationService* component which is based on the open source template-engine *Velocity* (Velocity, 2007). This component mirrors the reference model's *Message Renderer* entity described in Section 3.5.1.9.

- *RuleBase*: The *RuleBase* is the central repository for maintaining the CAITL-IM rules (cf. Section 4.2). It provides methods for creating, updating, and deleting these rules. The rules are persisted using XML (cf. Section 3.5.2.4). The *RuleBase* component provides functionalities for persisting and accessing the rules in an object-oriented way. The *RuleBase* corresponds to the reference model's *Rule Repository* (cf. Section 3.5.1.1).

4.3.2.2 MessagingServiceClient

The *MessagingServiceClient* (MSC) provides graphical interfaces for both maintaining the CAITL-IM rules (cf. Section 4.2) and for using the value adding services introduced above. The first, a high-level graphical wizard for creating CAITL rules provides a wizard for specifying the *Message Triggering Situation* (cf. Section 3.4.6) and its associated *Message Type Body* (cf. 3.4.1). For specifying the *Message Triggering Situation* the *query by forms* (Halpin, 2001) technique is tailored according to the requirements of CAITL. The strengths of the modified approach are flexibility and extensibility; for example, a new condition statement (cf. Sections 3.5.2.4 and 4.2) can be added to the wizard by simply adding a configuration statement, i.e., the wizard can be extended without the need to modify the underlying source code; for details refer to Wachter (2008). A slightly modified version of the proposed wizard, which is based on XML configurations, was successfully employed for situation-based sending of SMS messages within the *ilbi* project (ilbi, 2008) further emphasizing the practicality of this approach.

The MSC was implemented based on the *Eclipse Rich Client Platform* (Eclipse Foundation, 2008a). Related screenshots of the MSC are presented in Section 4.4.1.5.

4.3.3 Innsbruck.mobile – Deployment View

The *deployment view*[23] illustrates the physical environment of *innsbruck.mobile* using a UML *Deployment Diagram* (see Figure 53):

---

[23] This view is also known as *physical view* (IEEE, 2000)

4.3 CAIPS-IM: Architecture

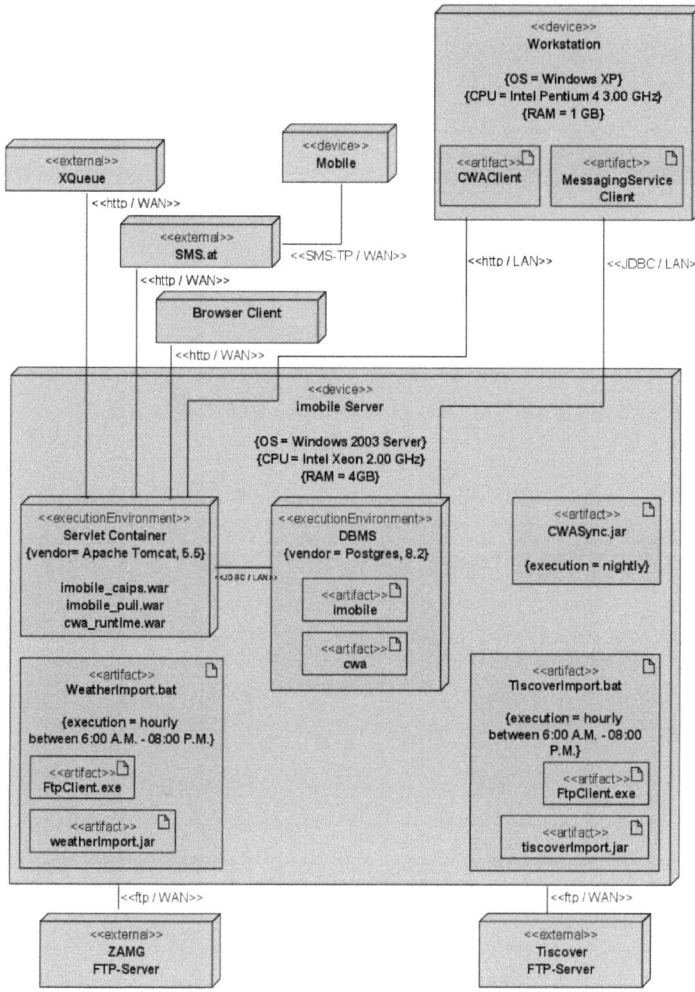

Figure 53: Deployment Diagram *innsbruck.mobile*

The deployment diagram depicts a static view of the runtime configuration of the system's hardware and the software deployed on this hardware. For a better understanding the diagram includes external third party systems as well as the clients employed by the end-users' (i.e., browser and mobile device). As described in Section 4.3.1, *innsbruck.mobile* is fundamentally composed of two subsystems namely, the *push* (i.e., CAIPS-IM) and the *pull* subsystem. The server-side components of these two subsystems are implemented drawing on the *Java Servlet* technology and are deployed on the *Apache Tomcat* servlet container (Apache Software Foundation, 2008). The server-side part of the *CWA* recommender subsystem is running in that container as well. The two associated databases *imobile* (cf. Section 4.3.1) and *cwa* are deployed on the *PostgreSQL* DBMS (PostgreSQL Global Development Group, 2008). The latter stores the problem solving knowledge of the underlying *CWA* subsystem (cf. Section 4.3.1.1) such as the filter rules, the product model, the user model, or deduction rules.

The data access services are implemented as standalone Java applications drawing on traditional ftp client software. These services (*TiscoverImport* and *WeatherImport*) as well as the *Apache Tomcat* servlet container are running on the *imobile* server. Moreover, the synchronization service ensuring consistency between the recommender's internal database (*cwa*) and the *imobile* database is running on that server as well.

The corresponding client software namely, the *MessagingServiceClient* (cf. Section 4.3.2.2) and the *CWAClient* (cf. Section 4.3.1) are deployed on a workstation.

4.4 Qualitative Evaluation

The requirements posed by CAIPS (cf. Section 3.3) provide the basis for assessing the conceptual framework introduced in Section 3.5. CAIPS-IM was implemented based on this conceptual framework. Its architecture (cf. Section 4.3) as well as the applied context-aware information triggering language CAITL-IM (cf. Section 4.2) were derived from the respective counterpart of the conceptual framework, namely the reference model (cf. Section 3.5.1) and the modular language framework (cf. Section 3.5.2) respectively.

Based on CAIPS-IM's architecture and the employed *Message Types* (cf. Section 4.2) it is qualitatively evaluated whether CAIPS-IM meets the requirements posed by CAIPS (cf. Section 3.3). Due to the fact, that CAIPS-IM was derived from the conceptual framework it can be inferred that, if CAIPS-IM meets the appropriate requirements, the conceptual framework fulfills these requirements as well. Similar to Section 3.3 the evaluation is classified according to the stakeholders. The requirements posed by the service provider are evaluated in Section 4.4.1, the requirements posed by the user are evaluated in Section 4.4.2.

It is worth noting that in addition to CAIPS-IM, the implementation of *ilbi* (ilbi, 2008) was also partially based on the conceptual framework (cf. Section 3.5) which furthermore demonstrates its practicability. Within the *ilbi* project, which is focused on sending location-based messages with predefined content, fundamental concepts of the conceptual framework were successfully implemented. For example, the concept of a *Message Triggering Situation* for determining appropriate message receivers as well as a corresponding wizard (also based on the modified query by forms approach, cf. Section 4.3.2.2) were successfully implemented.

4.4.1 Service Provider Requirements

4.4.1.1 Automatic Message Delivery

Automatic, i.e., situation-based message delivery requires a mechanism for specifying situations whose occurrence triggers the sending of the associated information. This requirement is well supported as it is the fundamental functionality of CAIPS. CAIPS employs the concept of a *Message Triggering Situation* to specify such a condition (cf. Section 3.4.6). The occurrence of such a situation in turn leads to the creation of a *Message Instance* (cf. Section 3.4.4) and its associated *Final Message* (cf. Section 3.4.5) which is automatically sent to the appropriate user. The *Message Triggering Situation* is specified exploiting CAITL's event and condition part. Its modular structure, i.e., CAITL's support of different subscription and query languages for specifying the event and condition part enables a very powerful specification of the MTS; its expressiveness can be customized by adequately choosing and combining subscription and query languages. In CAITL-IM the subscription language "imobile_sl" (cf. Section 4.2) and the "Hibernate Query Language" (cf. Hibernate, 2007) are employed for specifying the *Message Triggering Situation*.

4.4.1.2 Situation Dependent Message Content Definition

This requirement asks for a specification of a message's content (i.e., the *Message Type Body*) dependent on a *Message Triggering Situation*. This requirement is directly addressed by the rule language as well. While the event and condition parts are exploited for describing the MTS the action part specifies the content of a message, i.e., it defines the *Message Type Body* (cf. Section 3.4.1). The discussion of CAITL's global semantics (cf. Section 3.5.2.3) has shown the direct relationship of a rule's event and condition part with its action part; hence, the *Message Triggering Situation* (defined by CAITL's event and condition part) is directly associated with the *Message Type Body* (defined by CAITL's action part). The communication between both parts is realized using communication variables (cf. Section 3.5.2.5) enabling the incorporation of MTS specific information into the IVCI retrieval process (cf. Section 3.5.1.3).

4.4.1.3 Automatic Personalization

This requirement asks for personalized messages. It is addressed by a two-tiered customization process. First, the knowledge-based recommender system CWA (cf. Section 4.3.1.1) is exploited for determining the *Information Value Chain Instances* most relevant for the user in his current situation. They are determined according to the *Information Value Chain Concepts* specified in the associated *Message Type* (cf. Section 3.5.1.3). Second, an appropriate *Final Message* is rendered for each of the user's preferred communication channels (cf. *AdaptationService* in Section 4.3.2.1).

4.4.1.4 Extensibility

This requirement asks for support in creating new *Message Types*. This requirement is perfectly met by the rule language CAITL-IM (cf. Section 4.2) as it enables to declaratively create new *Message Types* and associate them with appropriate MTSs. The process of creating *Message Types* exploiting a CAITL is summarized in Section 3.1.

4.4.1.5 Ease-of-Use

This requirement asks for tool support facilitating the rule creation process, i.e., to relieve the service provider of being forced to create rules directly using the CAITL syntax. As already stated in Dey (2001), the tradeoff between expressing complex contextual situations and providing a simple method for describing these situations is hard to solve. CAIPS tackles this

4.4 Qualitative Evaluation

challenge both through an intuitive *Message Triggering Situation* approach (exploiting CAITL's intuitive semantics based on E-C-A rules) and a wizard providing a high-level interface for creating CAITL rules by a few *clicks* only. Subsequently, the five tiered rule creation process is exemplified by creating the "Good Morning Message" *Message Type* using the wizard as implemented for CAIPS-IM (cf. Section 4.3.2.2). In the first step general information regarding the *Message Type* is specified, e.g. a label, a description, or type specific parameters such as user individual delivery times (see Figure 54):

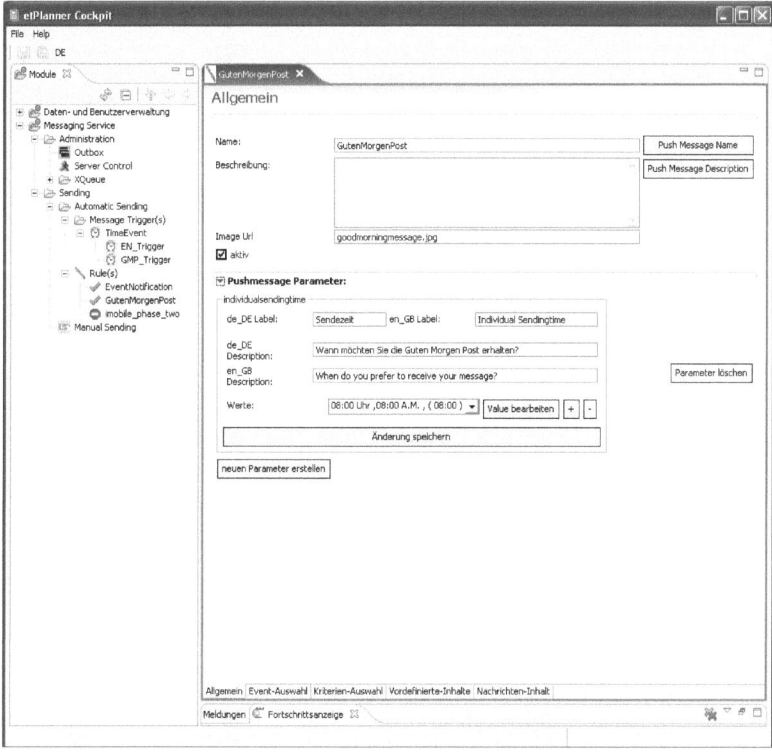

Figure 54: Rule Creation – General Information

This information is exploited for dynamically creating the corresponding subscription interfaces (cf. Section 4.4.2.1). In the next step the rule's event part, i.e., the event subscription (cf. Section 3.5.2.4) is created by choosing a subscription statement from a drop-down list. The selectable elements, i.e., the subscription statements can be created using the rule wizard as well. It depends on the subscription (i.e., whether one subscribes for an internal or external event, cf. Section 3.5.1.5) whether an *EventGenerator* (cf. Section 4.3.2.1) and its corresponding subscription statement are created or solely a subscription statement.

This process is illustrated in Figure 55 showing the creation of an *EventGenerator* publishing internal events, namely temporal events. In this case both an *EventGenerator* reporting the reaching of specific points of time and the corresponding subscription statement are created.

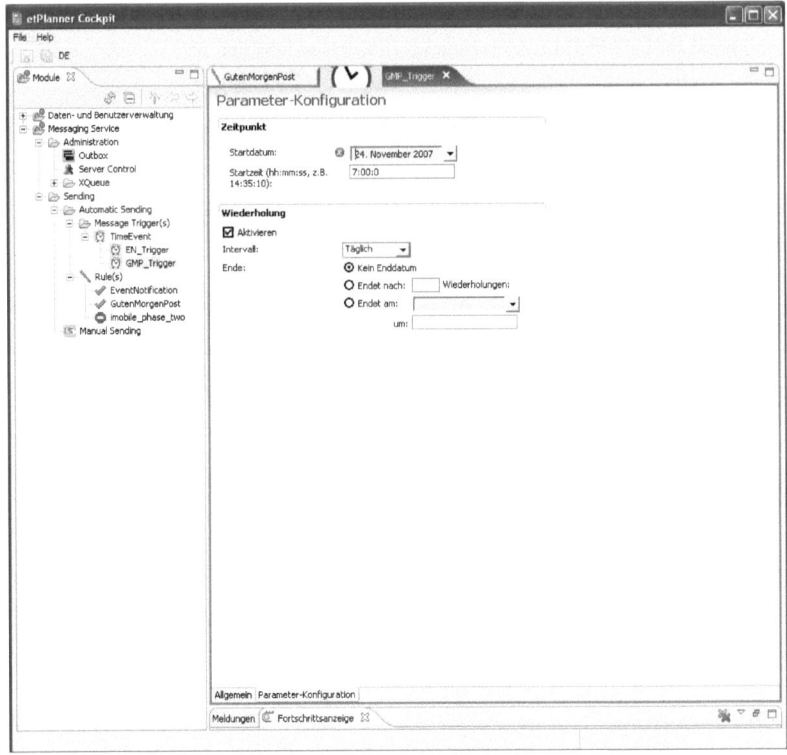

Figure 55: Rule Creation – Publisher & Corresponding Subscription Creation

In the third step the specification of the Message Triggering Situation is completed by defining appropriate constraints further restricting the number of potential message receivers. As discussed in Section 4.3.2.2, this is realized by a modified query by forms technique, i.e., the service provider selects a query and modifies it to fit the particular situation. The corresponding query statement, i.e., the HQL statement is generated according to the selected form fields. Experienced users may directly edit the query statement. An example query selecting all users subscribed for the *Good Morning Message* is illustrated in Figure 56:

4.4 Qualitative Evaluation

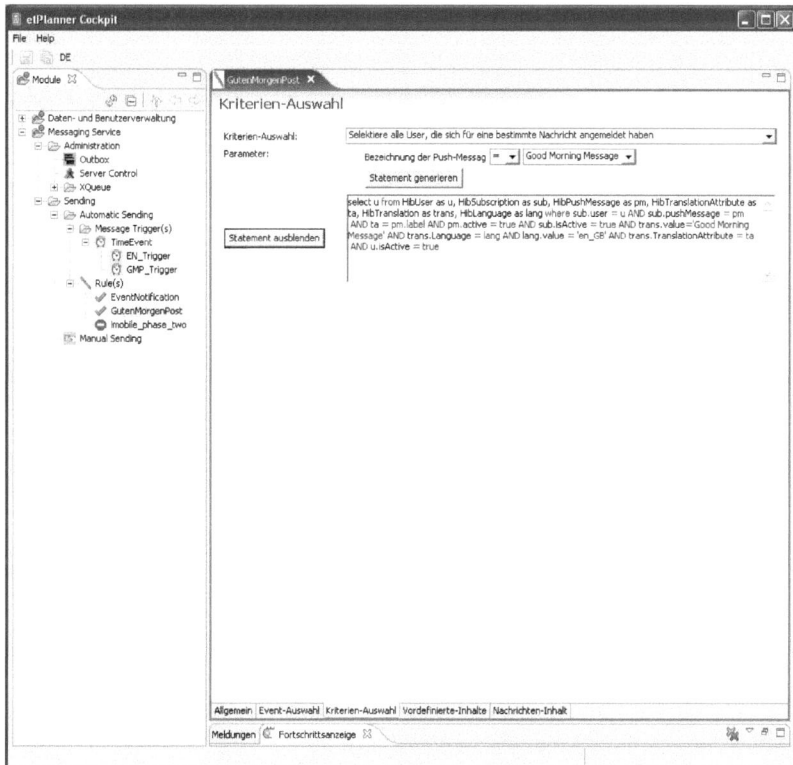

Figure 56: Rule Creation – Condition Part

In the next step the *Information Value Chain Concepts* (cf. Section 3.4.2) comprised in the *Message Type* and appropriate configuration information of the corresponding recommender and/or selector components are specified (cf. Section 4.2), i.e., the rule's action part is created (see Figure 57):

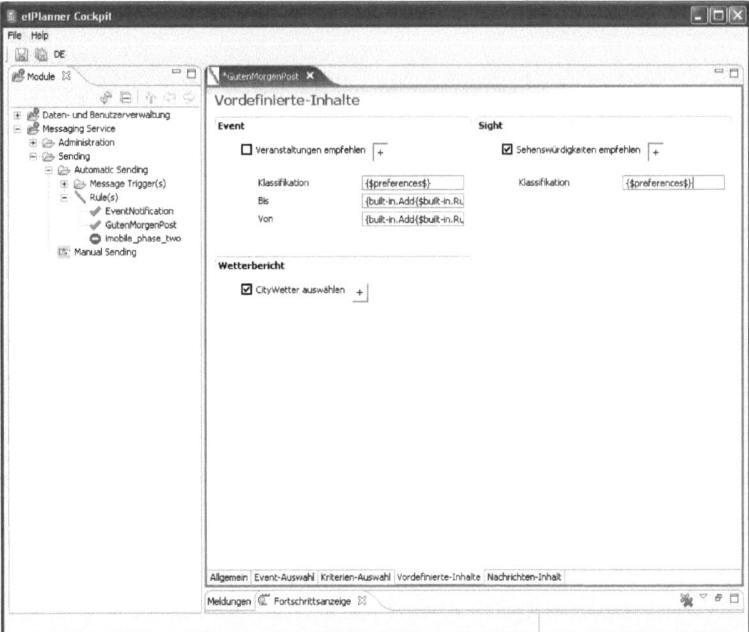

Figure 57: Rule Creation – Action Part (IVCCs)

In the fifth and final step the message templates for the two supported communication channels, i.e., e-mail and SMS are created (see Figure 58):

4.4 Qualitative Evaluation   119

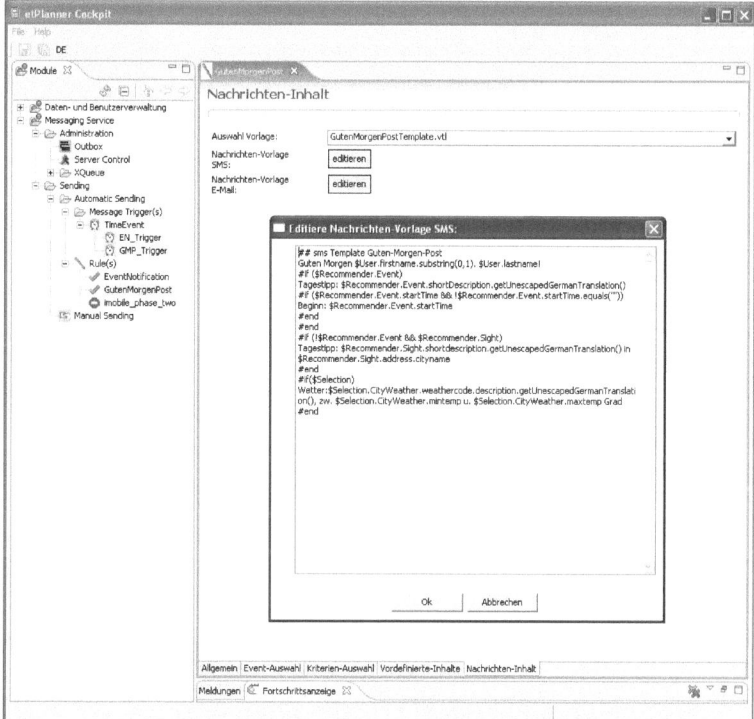

Figure 58: Rule Creation – Action Part (Template)

4.4.1.6 Multiple Communication Channels

This requirement asks for the support of different communication channels. In the case of CAIPS-IM SMS and e-mail communication channels are provided. This requirement is tackled by the proposed concepts of *Message Instance* and *Final Message* (cf. sections 3.4.4 and 3.4.5 respectively). Their successful implementation within CAIPS-IM has demonstrated the applicability of these concepts.

4.4.2 User Requirements

4.4.2.1 Expressive Subscription Specification

This requirement asks for an expressive subscription mechanism for the information needs of the users. A user may state his information needs in two steps: First, he subscribes to desired *Message Type(s)* (hence, he states his interest in the information provided by that *Message Type*, cf. channel based subscription in Section 2.3.2.3). Additionally, he may provide *Message Type* specific information such as an individual delivery time. Second, the user states his preferences regarding the *Information Value Chain Concepts* which are comprised in the corresponding *Message Type*. The respective user interfaces are illustrated in Figure 59 and Figure 60 respectively:

Figure 59: Information Needs – Type Subscription

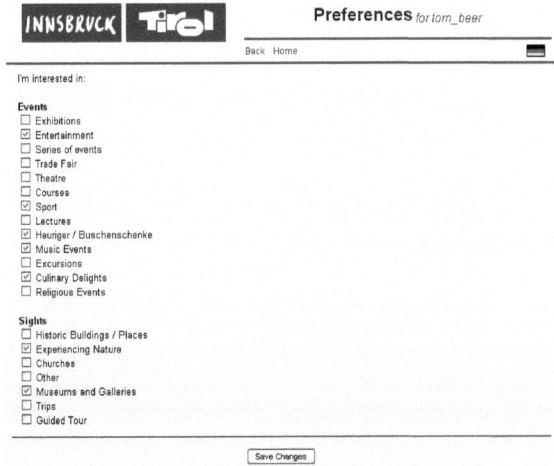

Figure 60: Information Needs – Preferences Elicitation

4.4 Qualitative Evaluation

4.4.2.2 Practical Subscription Interfaces

This requirement asks for subscription interfaces automatically adapting to the employed devices. This requirement is not addressed by CAIPS itself; it is rather addressed by the etPlanner framework which focuses on adapting its user interfaces to the user's context (Höpken et al., 2008).

4.4.2.3 Avoid Similar Message Content

This requirement asks for a mechanism to avoid multiple sending of the same *Final Message* in the same *Message Triggering Situation*. CAIPS provides two solutions for this problem. First, elaborate subscription languages are supported enabling the systematic selection of occurring events. Second, both the *Message Type Body*, i.e., the contained *Information Value Chain Instances* and the corresponding *Message Triggering Situation* are "logged" and may be regarded as contextual information as well (cf. Section 4.1). Therefore, this historic information can be incorporated into the condition statement as well as into the *Information Value Chain Instance* retrieval mechanism. The latter avoids providing the same *Information Value Chain Instance* multiple times by incorporating the historic information into the recommender's filtering rules (cf. Section 4.3.1.1).

5 Related Work

> *It is not once nor twice but times without number that the same ideas make their appearance in the world*
>
> Aristotle (384 - 322 BC)

This section reviews related approaches; both, similar systems enabling context-aware information delivery and frameworks supporting the development of context-aware systems are considered. Context-awareness is subject of a number of research areas ranging from research in ontology languages to software engineering. The former primarily deals with context modeling whereas the latter is focused on the design and development of infrastructures and frameworks facilitating the implementation of context-aware systems. Numerous such engineering approaches have been proposed over the last decade. Due to the huge number, this thesis is focused on those which enable the rule-based exploitation of gathered context information. Subsequently, each of the examined approaches is briefly introduced and contrasted to CAIPS. The results are summarized in Section 5.5.

5.1 SOCAM

5.1.1 Overview

The *service-oriented context-aware middleware* (*SOCAM*) research project (Gu et al., 2004a; Gu et al., 2004c) proposes an infrastructure for building and rapidly prototyping context-aware services. It converts *physical spaces* into *semantic spaces* enabling context-aware services to easily access the transformed context information.

SOCAM was developed on top of the *Open Service Gateway Initiative (OSGi)* which provides a lightweight framework for delivering and executing service-oriented applications (OSGi Alliance, 2008). The underlying ontology-based context model was specified using OWL (Antoniou & van Harmelen, 2004; Lacy, 2005; McGuinness & van Harmelen, 2004). One of *SOCAM*'s key features is its support for reasoning over various context information such as deriving high-level from low-level and implicit from explicit ones. Two different kinds of reasoning are supported, namely *ontology* and *user-defined* reasoning. The former supports all specifications inherently provided by OWL Lite and RDFS such as disjointness and cardinality. The latter provides a rule-based facility for deducing higher-level context states. Both forward & backward chaining and a hybrid mode which combines the two approaches are supported. *SOCAM*'s architecture is composed of the following distributed components which are designed as independent service components:

- *Context provider*: Provide abstractions of the heterogeneous low-level context sources using OWL.
- *Service-locating service*: Add-on service for locating context providers.
- *Context interpreter*: May be considered as another *context provider* which provides high-level contexts by interpreting and reasoning over low-level contexts. It is composed of a context reasoner and a context knowledge base storing ontology information (both T-Box and A-Box information).
- *Context-aware application*: Strictly speaking, this component is not part of the architecture. It is rather the context-aware application itself which is developed based on the service components introduced above. The implementation is supported by the capability to specify conditional clauses which allow the invocation of predefined methods under certain conditions. These rules are stored in a file and preloaded into the context reasoner.

5.1.2 Discussion

On the face of it, there are some similarities between *SOCAM* and CAIPS suggested by *SOCAM's* capability to employ a kind of production rules for building context-aware applications. Even if these rules may be exploited for defining contextual situations, their expressiveness is heavily restricted. On the contrary, CAIPS employs elaborate component languages enabling the rich specification of contextual situations. For example, subscription languages enable the expression of temporal relations between occurring events supporting an elaborate handling of duplicate instances (cf. Section 2.3.4). Such a mechanism is of special interest within context-aware systems to avoid the unintended, multiple firing of rules (cf. Section 3.4.7).

5.2 SE Framework for Context-Aware Pervasive Computing

5.2.1 Overview

Henricksen and Indulska (2004) propose a conceptual framework and software infrastructure for facilitating the prototyping of context-aware applications (*SEF*). Contrasted to the SOCAM approach (cf. Section 5.1) this work is rather focused on conceptual tasks such as context modeling and programming models than on architectural issues. One of its key components is the *Context Modeling Language* (CML), a notation technique for graphically modeling context. The language provides modeling primitives for describing *fact types* (e.g., a person), their *dependencies*, their *classifications* (i.e., whether they are sensed, static, profiled, or derived), and *quality metadata* (e.g., probabilistic measures indicating the certainty of a user's location). It moreover supports the specification of constraints such as *cardinalities*, *relationships*, or *lifetime constraints of historical facts*[24]. CML itself is based on the *Object-Role Modeling* (ORM[25]) approach which provides a conceptual modeling method (Brodie et al., 1984) close to natural language, i.e., it expresses the corresponding model in terms of natural concepts such as objects and roles. For details regarding ORM it is referred to Halpin (2001). One of the strengths of ORM is its capability to seamlessly map the conceptual model to the relational model which in turn is well suited for efficient querying tasks.

They introduce the concept of *situation abstraction* supporting the representation of high-level contexts, i.e., the expression of situations employing a decidable fragment of predicate logic[26]. Hence, enabling for example, the specification of the situation that a person is engaged and must not be interrupted, using the high-level context predicate *occupied*.

Furthermore, the framework comprises a *triggering* programming model which supports the implementation of reactive behavior, i.e., it facilitates the automatic invocation of actions in response to context changes exploiting the event-condition-action paradigm (cf. Section 2.1.2.2).

A corresponding event is represented by a context change which in turn is described as a change in a situation state (cf. situation abstraction which is described above). There are three possible situation states, namely *true*, *false*, or *unknown* and six distinct state transitions (i.e., enterSTATE, exitSTATE). An event may be associated with any of these transitions. Similar to

---

[24] fact types may be annotated whether historical context information is retained
[25] It is important not to mistake this abbreviation for the identical abbreviation for *object relational mapping*
[26] The concept of situation abstraction may be compared with that of CybreMinder (cf. Section 5.3). However, its expressiveness is considerably higher.

the event, a condition is specified employing situation predicates. The corresponding action specifies the methods to be invoked using programming languages such as Java directly.

In addition to the conceptual framework a software infrastructure providing runtime support for the proposed programming models and context management was partially implemented. The infrastructure is composed of loosely coupled layers which are described below:

- *Context gathering layer*: Responsible for acquisition of context information from physical and logical sensors. The raw context data are processed based on interpretation and aggregation techniques.
- *Context reception layer*: Provides a bidirectional interface between the gathering and the management layer. It transforms the heterogeneous information of the former into the fact abstraction of the latter. Each fact type is represented by a receptor component performing the interaction between both layers, i.e., posing queries, and/or creating appropriate event subscriptions.
- *Context management layer*: Acts as a repository for storing context models and their instantiations employing a relational database.
- *Query layer*: Provides the higher layers with a convenient interface for querying the context repository based on fact and situation abstractions. Three types of queries are supported: *fact queries*, *situation queries*, and *event queries*
- *Adaptation layer*: Supports the branching and triggering programming model; for example, it manages trigger definitions and evaluates these on behalf of the application layer based on the functionality of the query layer.
- *Application layer:* Provides further support for both programming models by offering a toolkit which developers may exploit for developing their own context-aware applications.

5.2.2 Discussion

The focus of *SEF* is to provide a conceptual framework as well as an infrastructure for prototyping context aware applications. Therefore, it should not be directly contrasted with CAIPS. However, some of the proposed concepts are similar to those applied in CAIPS. In particular, the triggering model is worth discussing in greater detail.

The focus of the proposed triggering model is the support of programming in an asynchronous style, i.e., to support prototyping of applications which need to immediately react on context changes such as location-based applications. Similar to CAITL, the proposed triggering model is based on the event-condition-action paradigm. However, the corresponding approaches differ in the expressiveness. For example, CAITL supports the employment of event algebras using appropriate subscription languages (cf. Sections 2.3.4 and 3.5.2.2) to specify rich event subscriptions, whereas *SEF* is restricted to simple sequences and sets of alternative state transitions (cf. *temporal disjunctive* and *temporal sequence* operator respectively, see Section 2.3.4). Furthermore, CAITL's modular design supports different context modeling techniques (cf. Section 3.5.2.2). *SEF*, in contrast, is tailored to ORM and the corresponding implementation using relational databases.

The proposed triggering model sounds interesting, however, it seems to be purely academic as a proof of concept is missing (even in later work, cf. Henricksen & Indulska (2006)).

5.3 CybreMinder

5.3.1 Overview

CybreMinder (Dey & Abowd, 2000a) is a Java based application which was developed based on the *Context Toolkit* (Dey et al., 2001). Its focus is the support of users in sending and receiving context enriched reminders, for example, to remember a user to take his umbrella to work when he leaves his apartment. The reminders can be provided via three different communication channels, namely SMS, e-mail, and nearby displays. A reminder's creation process involves two steps: First, similar to e-mail creation the recipient(s), a subject, a message text, a priority, and an expiration timestamp are specified. Second, the created reminder message is associated with a situation defining when the reminder has to be delivered. To do so the user is assisted with a graphical interface supporting him in creating appropriate situations by refining pre-defined name-value pairs. After finishing the situation creation process the reminder is sent. If no situation is attached to the reminder it is immediately delivered to the specified user(s). Otherwise, the reminder is delivered at future time when the situation can be satisfied. Before the reminder is delivered the most appropriate communication channel for each recipient is determined. By default, the reminder is provided to the closest display. However, the users can also specify their preferred communication channel.

The evaluation of the specified situations is realized within an *aggregator* component. This component aggregates all pieces of context concerning a particular entity such as a person. The aggregator manages the interaction with other involved components (such as widgets) and determines when a delivery situation has occurred. Moreover, it is responsible to monitor expired reminders. An expired reminder is sent to both the potential receiver and the sender along with the information that the reminder has been expired.

5.3.2 Discussion

At first glance, there are significant similarities between CAIPS and the *CybreMinder* prototype. These similarities are mainly caused by the fact that *CybreMinder* automatically sends messages depending on a prespecified situation. However, these messages are restricted to textual reminders and are of static nature. As its focus is on sending and receiving textual reminders exclusively it does not support the creation of personalized, tailored messages as realized in CAIPS.

Similar to CAIPS *CybreMinder* employs the concept of a "triggering situation" to specify when the associated reminder has to be delivered. Contrasted to CAIPS, however, this approach offers a considerably limited expressiveness to specify this triggering situation. Its specification is restricted to key/value comparisons. CAIPS, on the other hand, employs a combination of subscription and query languages which enables the specification of expressive *Message Triggering Situations* (cf. Section 3.4.6).

Moreover, *CybreMinder's* specification of the triggering situation is tightly bound to the corresponding context representation, i.e., key/value pairs. The drawbacks of key/value based context representations are discussed in Section 2.2.1. CAIPS, on the other hand, supports arbitrary context modeling approaches (cf. Section 3.5.2).

5.4 COMPASS

5.4.1 Overview

COMPASS is an acronym for *Context-aware Mobile Personal ASSistant* which describes the concept of a context-aware mobile tourist guide providing tourists with information (such as buddy lists and nearby buildings) according to their current situation. Its implementation is based on context-aware and recommender systems (van Setten et al., 2004).

One of its fundamental components is a map showing the user's current location and a selection of nearby buildings and buddies. The displayed objects are updated when the user moves. The objects are linked with web-services enabling, for example, to reserve a table in a restaurant or booking tickets for an event. The displayed objects are retrieved in a three-tiered process. First, the underlying platform retrieves search services according to the hard facts of the user's context (e.g., the tourist's current location). Second, these services (e.g. search services for museums) are exploited to retrieve items matching the hard facts of the user's context. Subsequently, the retrieved objects are ranked using a recommender system.

The underlying architecture is composed of four basic building blocks. The first is composed of third party services, namely network services such as messaging services, context services such as location providers, and business services such as providers of restaurant menus. The second is built by middleware services such as service registries and context managers. The service registry provides ontology based access services for third party services. The context manager can be compared to a *Context Provider* (cf. Section 3.5.1.7). The third is represented by the application itself providing an interaction manager and a POI retriever. The fourth is an external recommender service which is responsible for ranking the previously retrieved POIs exploiting object specific prediction strategies (cf. recommendation strategy in Section 2.4).

5.4.2 Discussion

COMPASS describes an application which integrates context-aware and recommender systems within a mobile tourist guide to provide the tourists with suitable buildings nearby. Its focus is on an open platform allowing the easy integration of the contributing services.

Except for the exploitation of recommender and context-aware systems COMPASS and CAIPS are quite different, i.e., the objectives posed by these systems are different. Referring to Dey and Abowd (2000b) COMPASS may be considered as a typical representative of the *presentation* system category (cf. Section 2.2.1). A CAIPS, however, may be considered as an application combining the features of *presentation* and *context-triggered actions* (cf. Section 2.2.1). A detailed evaluation of *COMPASS* is presented in Schwinger et al. (2005).

5.5 Summary

This section summarizes the discussed systems and frameworks. The following criteria are used for comparison:

- **Extensibility (EXT):** This criterion shows whether the system supports the creation of new *Message Types*, i.e., whether it is restricted to a specific *Message Type* such as reminder messages.
- **Multiple Communication Channels (MCC):** This criterion shows whether the system supports different communication channels for message delivery.
- **Personalized Message Content (PMC):** This criterion shows whether the system provides personalized, i.e., user related information.
- **Situation Dependent Messaging (SDM):** This criterion shows whether the system supports the specification of a situation whose occurrence triggers the message delivery process (cf. *Message Triggering Situation* in Section 3.4.6).
- **Configurable SDM (CON):** This criterion shows whether the triggering situation is configurable, i.e., whether it can be declaratively specified.
- **Expressiveness SDM (EXP):** This criterion rates the expressiveness of the mechanism exploited for specifying the *Message Triggering Situation*. (scale: low, medium, high)
- **Independence from the Context Representation Technology (IND):** This criterion shows whether the system supports different context representation technologies.

Based on these criteria, the systems, which were discussed in the previous sections, are contrasted in Table 8:

5.5 Summary

	SOCAM	SEF	CybreMinder	COMPASS	CAIPS
EXT	N/A	N/A	no	no	yes
MCC	N/A	N/A	SMS, e-mail, nearby displays	no	yes
PMC	N/A	N/A	no	yes	yes
SDM	yes	yes	yes	yes	yes
CON	conditional clauses	triggering model (E-C-A)	conditional clauses	no	E-C-A
EXP	low/medium	medium/high	low	N/A	high
IND	no	no	no	no	yes

Table 8: Related Work – Overview

As the table shows, none of the discussed systems supports the creation of new *Message Types*. Rather, the observed systems are restricted to application specific *Message Types*. Different communication channels are supported by the CybreMinder application only. The creation of personalized messages, i.e., the delivery of tailored information which is highly relevant for the corresponding user, is supported by the COMPASS application only. All discussed systems and frameworks support situation dependent messaging, i.e., they support the specification of a situation whose occurrence triggers an appropriate action such as the creation and delivery of personalized messages. SOCAM, SEF, and CybreMinder support the declarative specification of such a situation applying conditional clauses (SOCAM and CybreMinder) and E-C-A rules (SEF). The expressiveness of the two approaches applying conditional clauses varies because of the underlying context representation. While SOCAM employs an OWL based context model, CybreMinder uses key/value pairs for representing context. The expressiveness of the SEF approach can be rated high, but the applied E-C-A rules are restricted to the underlying context representation technology. Neither SEF no any of the other discussed frameworks and systems support different context representation technologies. Summarizing, CAIPS is the only system which excellently satisfies all of the comparison criteria.

6 Conclusion

The whole is simpler than the sum of its parts

Willard Gibbs (1839 - 1903)

This section concludes the thesis. First, the research presented in this thesis and its major contributions are outlined in Section 6.1. Second, future work and open issues are discussed in Section 6.2.

6.1 Summary

The focus of this thesis is the design of a conceptual framework facilitating the implementation of context-aware information push systems (CAIPS). A context-aware push system, as proposed in this thesis, enables its operator to declaratively provide the users with tailored information related to their current situation and preferences. The conceptual framework is fundamentally composed of a *reference model* and a *rule language framework*. The applicability of the conceptual framework is demonstrated by the implementation of a specific context-aware information push system, namely CAIPS-IM. CAIPS-IM was "derived" from the conceptual framework and is developed as an integrated part of the mobile tourist guide *innsbruck.mobile*.

The first section of this thesis presented an introductory usage scenario from the tourism domain. Moreover, this section provided the rationale for building CAIPS drawing on both a study determining the attitude of potential end-users towards such a system and typical application scenarios from tourism. Furthermore, the key contributions of this thesis were discussed within this section; they are summarized subsequently:

- a detailed discussion of the fundamental techniques behind CAIPS (i.e., knowledge representation, expert systems, context-aware systems, publish/subscribe systems, and recommender systems)
- the development of the conceptual framework facilitating the design and implementation of domain independent, declarative, context-aware information push systems

- a novel publish/subscribe approach producing tailored messages on demand
- a case study of the design and implementation of CAIPS-IM, a context-aware information push system implemented as an integrated part of the mobile tourist information system *innsbruck.mobile*. Its implementation was fundamentally based on the proposed conceptual framework.

The next section (Section 2) introduced the core techniques behind CAIPS, namely knowledge representation & expert systems, context-aware systems, publish/subscribe systems, and recommender systems. Both their collaboration and their roles within CAIPS were discussed, i.e., it was shown how they contribute to the conceptual framework. Knowledge representation and expert systems heavily influenced the design of CAIPS, therefore, they were discussed in greater detail. Referring to Davis et al. (1993) the meaning of the former was discussed in terms of five roles. Moreover, the knowledge types as applied within CAIPS, namely declarative and procedural knowledge as well as corresponding representation technologies (i.e., object-oriented, rules, and ontologies) were introduced. Furthermore, the principles and the architecture of expert systems were discussed. Subsequently, expert systems were contrasted with techniques appearing similar to expert systems, namely rule-based systems, the business rules approach, relational databases, and knowledge-based systems. Contributing system architectures, namely these of context-aware, publish/subscribe, and recommender systems were examined. In addition to architectural issues context modeling, subscription languages, and recommendation strategies were discussed. Hence, this section provided the theoretically background for the development of the conceptual framework of CAIPS.

This conceptual framework was described in detail in Section 3. It facilitates the design and implementation of context-aware information push systems by providing a *reference model* and a *rule language framework*.

The reference model specifies the fundamental functional and logical parts of CAIPS. The reference model shows that a number of *base systems*, namely, expert, publish/subscribe, context-aware, and recommender systems (cf. Section 2) is well suited for building CAIPS.

The rule language framework supports the development of specific context-aware information triggering languages. Such a reactive rule language enables the declarative specification of *Message Types* and their association with *Message Triggering Situations*. It was shown that the combination of object-oriented or ontology-based and rule representation technologies perfectly fulfills the requirement of representing both declarative and procedural knowledge.

Prior to the description of the conceptual framework the requirements, which have to be met by context-aware information push systems, were defined. Moreover, this section:

- provided an overview of the key concepts behind CAIPS
- introduced the stakeholders of CAIPS
- provided relevant definitions

Section 4 described the design and implementation of a specific CAIPS system, namely CAIPS-IM drawing on the mobile tourist information system *innsbruck.mobile*. Its architecture was illustrated exploiting three views, namely the system overview, the conceptual, and the deployment view. Furthermore, the applied context-aware information triggering language CAITL-IM was introduced. Subsequently, the requirements defined in Section 3.3 were evaluated. The main objective of this evaluation was to prove the applicability of the conceptual framework. This was done by qualitatively evaluating the requirements drawing on CAIPS-IM. It was shown that the implementation of CAIPS-IM completely meets these requirements. Hence, as this implementation was derived from the conceptual framework it can be inferred that the conceptual framework fulfills these requirements as well.

Section 5 provided a survey of related systems. Although some of these systems could be exploited to support the development of context-aware information push systems this was not the task they were primarily developed for. It was shown that none of these approaches meet the requirements as posed by CAIPS.

6.2 Future Work

This thesis has tackled subjects related to several research areas ranging from context-aware computing to rule languages; due to this broad scope some issues are left for further examination. This section proposes future work in the following areas:

- *Implementation Framework*: This thesis proposed a conceptual framework facilitating the development of context-aware information push systems. Based on this conceptual, an implementation framework could be subject of future work. Such a framework is composed of already implemented functional modules; these may be customized to the system specific requirements by code extensions and/or appropriate configuration files. It has to be evaluated whether existing frameworks (mainly from the field of context-aware systems) could be extended and customized according to the requirements of CAIPS.
- *Security Issues*: CAIPS can be considered as a context-aware system; a characteristic these systems have in common is that they make heavily use of personal data. This personal information has to be prevented from misuse by third parties. The acceptance of context-aware systems – consequently of CAIPS – may be significantly influenced by the users' confidence in such systems. Therefore, methods for protecting this information have to be subject of future work.

- *Further Application Domains*: The instantiation of the conceptual framework was shown drawing on the mobile tourist guide *innsbruck.mobile*. However, the framework was designed independent of specific application domains; therefore, another subject of future work is the instantiation of the conceptual framework within further application domains. Such implementations will face new challenges and push the further development of CAIPS.

- *Business Model*: Future work may address the development of business models by identifying and quantifying benefits for the stakeholders in play. As a consequence the effectiveness of CAIPS as a novel communication and selling channel must be evaluated. Also the business models should be supported by appropriate market studies. The ultimate goal should be a profound estimation of the ROI for different application domains.

- *Implementing the context repository with alternative KR technologies*: Future work may evaluate the impacts of employing alternative knowledge representation technologies for the implementation of the *Context Repository*. For example, the design of the *Context Repository* indirectly influences the rule creation process. CAIPS, as implemented for the mobile tourist guide *innsbruck.mobile*, supports the service provider in creating rules by providing an appropriate wizard which is based on the *query by forms* technique. Employing ontology based storage and retrieval of context information may facilitate the rule creation process by enabling alternative wizard techniques such as ontology-based searching and browsing.

Bibliography

AAAI. (2008). AITopics/Representation [Electronic Version]. Retrieved 2008-03-06 from http://www.aaai.org/aitopics/pmwiki/pmwiki.php/AITopics/Representation.

G. D. Abowd, C. G. Atkeson, J. Hong, S. Long, R. Kooper & M. Pinkerton. (1997). Cyberguide: A mobile context-aware tour guide. *Wireless Networks, 3*(5), 421-433.

F. Adelstein, S. K. S. Gupta, G. Richard III & L. Schwiebert. (2005). *Fundamentals of Mobile and Pervasive Computing*: McGraw-Hill New York.

G. Adomavicius & A. Tuzhilin. (2001). *Multidimensional Recommender Systems: A Data Warehousing Approach.* Conference Proceedings of the Second Internatinal Workshop Electronic Commerce (WELCOM '01).

G. Adomavicius & A. Tuzhilin. (2005). Toward the Next Generation of Recommender Systems: A Survey of the State-of-the-Art and Possible Extensions. *IEEE Transactions on Knowledge and Data Engineering, 17*(6), 734-749.

M. Alavi & D. E. Leidner. (2005). Review: Knowledge Management and Knowledge Management Systems: Conceptual Foundations and Research Issues. In I. Nonaka (Ed.), *Knowledge Management - Critical Perspectives On Business And Management*: Taylor & Francis.

J. J. Alferes, R. Amador, E. Behrends, M. Berndtsson, F. Bry, G. Dawelbait, A. Doms, M. Eckert, O. Fritzen, W. May, P.-L. Patranjan, L. Royer, F. Schenk & M. Schroeder. (2005). *I5-D4, Specifcation of a Model, Language, and Architecture for Reactivity and Evolution.* Technical Report, Munic, Germany. REWERSE 6th Framework Programme.

M. Altinel & M. J. Franklin. (2000). *Efficient Filtering of XML Documents for Selective Dissemination of Information.* Conference Proceedings of the 26th International Conference on Very Large Data Bases, Cairo, Egypt.

Amazon.com. (2008). http://www.amazon.com/. Retrieved 2008-04-22, 2008

S. Ambler. (2004). *The Object Primer Agile Model Driven Development with UML 2* (3rd Edition ed.): Cambridge University Press.

J. R. Anderson. (1981). *Cognitive Skills and Their Acquisition*: Lawrence Erlbaum Associates, Hillsdale, NJ.

J. R. Anderson & C. Lebiere. (1998). *The Atomic Components of Thought*: Lawrence Erlbaum Associates.

J. Angele & G. Lausen. (2004). Ontologies in F-logic. In S. Staab & R. Studer (Eds.), *Handbook on Ontologies*. Berlin, Heidelberg, New York: Springer.

G. Antoniou & F. van Harmelen. (2004). Web Ontology Language: OWL. In S. Staab & R. Studer (Eds.), *Handbook On Ontologies*. Karlsruhe: Springer.

Apache Software Foundation. (2007). HiveMind [Electronic Version], 1.1. Retrieved 2008-08-27 from http://hivemind.apache.org/.

Apache Software Foundation. (2008). Apache Tomcat [Electronic Version]. Retrieved 2008-12-22 from http://tomcat.apache.org/.

F. Baader, I. Horrocks & U. Sattler. (2004). Description Logics. In S. Staab & R. Studer (Eds.), *Handbook on Ontologies*. Karlsruhe: Springer.

J. Bacon, J. Bates, R. Hayton & K. Moody. (1996). *Using Events to Build Distributed Applications.* Conference Proceedings of the 7th. ACM SIGOPS European Workshop, Connemara, Eire.

J. Bacon, K. Moody, J. Bates, R. Hayton, C. Ma, A. McNeil, O. Seidel & M. Spiteri. (2000). Generic Support for Distributed Applications. *IEEE Comput., 33*(3), 68-76.

J. Bailey, F. Bry, M. Eckert & P. Patranjan. (2005). *Flavours of XChange, a Rule-Based Reactive Language for the (Semantic) Web*. Conference Proceedings of the Int. Conference on Rules and Rule Markup Languages for the Semantic Web, Galway, Ireland.

J. Bailey, A. Poulovassilis & P. Wood, T. (2002). *An event-condition-action language for XML*. Conference Proceedings of the Proceedings of the 11th international conference on World Wide Web, Honolulu, Hawaii, USA.

M. Balabanovic & Y. Shoham. (1997). Content-based, Collaborative Recommendation. *Communications of the ACM, 40*(3), 66-72.

M. Baldauf, S. Dustdar & F. Rosenberg. (2007). A Survey on Context-Aware Systems. *International Journal of Ad Hoc and Ubiquitous Computing, 2*(4), 263-277.

H. Balzert. (2001). *Lehrbuch der Sofware-Technik I* (Vol. 2. Auflage). Heidelberg, Berlin: Spektrum.

E. Baralis, S. Ceri & S. Paraboschi. (1998). Compile-time and runtime analysis of active behaviors. *IEEE Transactions on Knowledge and Data Engineering, 10*(3), 353-370.

V. E. Barker, D. E. O'Connor, J. Bachant & E. Soloway. (1989). Expert Systems for Configuration at Digital: XCON and Beyond. *Communications of the ACM, 32*(3), 298-318.

L. Bass, P. Clements & R. Kazman. (2003). *Software Architecture in Practice*. Amsterdam: Addison-Wesley.

J. Bates, J. Bacon, K. Moody & M. Spiteri. (1998, September). *Using events for the scalable federation of heterogeneous components*. Conference Proceedings of the 8th ACM SIGOPS European Workshop: Support for Composing Distributed Applications, Sintra, Portugal.

V. Bazinette, N. H. Cohen, M. R. Ebling, G. D. h. Hunt & H. Lei. (2001). *An Itelligent Notification System*. Technical Report, Yorktown Heights, NY, USA. IBM Research.

T. Beer. (2004). A Danger Warning System in the Automative Field Using Methods Based on Semantic Web and Knowledge Management (Master Thesis, Saarland University, German Research Center for Artificial Intelligence, Saarbrücken, Germany, 2004).

T. Beer, W. Höpken, D. Jannach, M. Jessenitschnig, S. Mey, J. Rasinger & M. Zanker. (2008). *etPlanner: Architektur Deliverable*. Technical Report, Innsbruck Austria. eTourism Competence Center Austria.

E. Behrends, O. Fritzen, W. May & D. Schubert. (2006). An ECA Engine for Deploying Heterogeneous Component Languages in the Semantic Web. *Lecture Notes in Computer Science, 4254*, 887-898.

C. Beierle & G. Kern-Isberner. (2003). *Methoden wissensbasierter Systeme*. Hagen: Vieweg.

M. Beigl. (2000). MemoClip: A location-based remembrance appliance *Personal and Ubiquitous Computing, 4*(4), 230-233.

R. Belotti, C. Decurtins, M. Grossniklaus, M. C. Norrie & A. Palinginis. (2005). Modelling Context for Information Environments. In *Ubiquitous Mobile Information and Collaboration Systems* (pp. 43-56): Springer Berlin / Heidelberg.

T. J. M. Bench-Capon, D. Castelli, F. Coenen, L. Devendeville-Brisoux, B. Eaglestone, N. Fiddian, A. Gray, A. Ligeza & A. Vermesan. (1998). *Validation, Verification and Integrity Issues in Expert and Database Systems*. Conference Proceedings of the Database and Expert Systems Applications, 9th International Conference, DEXA '98, Vienna, Austria.

M. Berndtsson & B. Calestam. (2003). Graphical Notations for Active Rules in UML and UML-A. *ACM SIGSOFT Software Engineering Notes, 28*(2).

T. Berners-Lee, S. Hawke & D. Conolly. (2004). Comparing Rule-Based Systems [Electronic Version]. Retrieved 2007-08-08 from http://www.w3.org/2000/10/swap/doc/rule-systems.

T. Berners-Lee, J. Hendler & O. Lassila. (2001). The Semantic Web. *Scientific American, 284*(5), 28-37.

T. Bieger. (2005). *Management von Destinationen, 6. Auflage*: Oldenbourg, München, Wien.

A. D. Birrell & B. J. Nelson. (1984). Implementing remote procedure calls. *ACM Transactions on Computer Systems, 2*(1), 39-59.

T. Blecker, G. Friedrich, B. Kaluza, N. Abdelkafi & G. Kreutler. (2005). *Information And Management Systems For Product Customization*: Springer.

D. G. Bobrow & T. Winograd. (1977). An Overview of KRL, a Knowledge Representation Language. *Cognitive Science, 1*(1), 3-46.

F. Bodendorf. (2005). Daten- und Wissensmanagement.

H. Boley & S. Tabet. (2007). RuleML Lattice of Sublanguages [Electronic Version]. Retrieved 2007-08-03 from http://www.ruleml.org.

A. Bonifati, S. Ceri & S. Paraboschi. (2001). *Pushing reactive services to XML repositories using active rules.* Paper presented at the 10th International Conference on World Wide Web.

R. J. Brachman. (1979). On the Epistemological Status of Semantic Networks. In N. V. Findler (Ed.), *Associative networks: representation and use of knowledge by computers* (pp. 3–50). New York: Academic Press.

R. J. Brachman & H. J. Levesque. (2004). *Knowledge Representation and Reasoning*. San Francisco: Morgan Kaufmann.

R. Breu. (2001). *Objektorientierter Softwareentwurf - Integration mit UML*: Springer.

M. L. Brodie, J. Mylopoulos & J. W. Schmidt. (1984). *On Conceptual Modelling: Perspectives from Artificial Intelligence, Databases, and Programming Languages*: Springer Verlag.

F. Bry & P.-L. Patranjan. (2005). *Reactivity on the web: paradigms and applications of the language XChange.* Paper presented at the ACM symposium on Applied computing.

B. G. Buchanan & R. O. Duda. (1982). *Principles of Rule-Based Expert Systems* (No. CS-TR-82-926). Technical Report, Stanford, CA, USA. Stanford University.

G. Buchanan & A. Hinze. (2005). *A generic alerting service for digital libraries.* Conference Proceedings of the ACM/IEEE-CS joint conference on Digital libraries, Denver, Co.

R. Burke. (2002). Hybrid Recommender Systems: Survey and Experiments. *User Modeling and User-Adapted Interactions, 12*(4), 331-370.

J. Carlson & B. Lisper. (2003). An Interval-Based Algebra for Restricted Event Detection. *Lecture Notes in Computer Science, 2791*, 121-133.

A. Carzaniga. (1998). *Architectures for an Event Notification Service Scalable to Wide-area Networks.* (Doctoral dissertation, Politecnico Di Milano, Milan, Italy, 1998).

A. Carzaniga, E. Di Nitto, D. S. Rosenblum & A. L. Wolf. (1998). *Issues in supporting event-based architectural styles.* Conference Proceedings of the Third International Workshop on Software Architecture (ISAW '98).

A. Carzaniga, D. S. Rosenblum & A. L. Wolf. (2000). *Achieving Scalability and Expressiveness in an Internet-Scale Event Notification Service.* Conference Proceedings of the 19 Annual ACM Symposium on Principles of Distributed Computing, Portland, Oregon, United States

A. Carzaniga, D. S. Rosenblum & A. L. Wolf. (2001). Design and evaluation of a wide-area event notification service. *ACM Transactions on Computer Systems, 19*(3), 332-383.

S. Chakravarthy, V. Krishnaprasad, E. Anwar & S. K. Kim. (1994). *Composite Events for Active Databases: Semantics, Contexts and Detection.* Conference Proceedings of the 20th International Conference on Very Large Data Bases, San Francisco, CA, USA.

S. Chakravarthy & D. Mishra. (1994). Snoop: An Expressive Event Specification Language for Active Databases. *Data & Knowledge Engineering, 14*(1), 1-26.

G. Chen & D. Kotz. (2000). *A Survey of Context-Aware Mobile Computing Research.* Technical Report, Hanover, NH. Darthmouth Computer Science.

H. Chen, T. Finin & A. Joshi. (2003). *Using OWL in a Pervasive Computing Broker.* Conference Proceedings of the Workshop on Ontologies in Open Agent Systems.

K. Cheverst, N. Davies, K. Mitchell, A. Friday & C. Efstratiou. (2000). Developing a Context-aware Electronic Tourist Guide: Some Issues and Experiences. *CHI Letters, 2*(1), 17-24.

K. Cheverst, K. Mitchell & N. Davies. (2001). *Investigating Context-aware Informaiton Push vs. Information Pull to Tourists.* Conference Proceedings of the MobileHCI'01 workshop on HCI with Mobile Devices, Lille, France.

J. Y. Choeh & H. J. Lee. (2008). Mobile Push Personalization and User Experience. In D. Jannach, M. Zanker & J. Konstan (Eds.), *AI Communications - Special issue on Recommender Systems*: IOS Press, to appear 2008/09.

M. Cilia, C. Bornhövd & A. P. Buchmann. (2001). *Moving Active Functionality from Centralized to Open Distributed Heterogeneous Environments.* Conference Proceedings of the Cooperative Information Systems (CoopIS '01), 9 thConference, Trento, Italy.

M. Cilia, L. Fiege, C. Haul, A. Zeidler & A. P. Buchmann. (2003). *Looking into the past: enhancing mobile publish/subscribe middleware.* Conference Proceedings of the 2nd international workshop on distributed event-based systems, San Diego, California.

P. Clements, F. Bachmann, L. Bass, D. Garlan, J. Ivers, R. Little, R. Nord & J. Stafford. (2002). *Documenting Software Architectures: Views and Beyond.* London, Munich, Paris: Addison-Wesley.

E. F. Codd. (1970). A relational model of data for large shared data banks. *Commun. ACM, 13*(6), 377-387.

A. Colmerauer & P. Roussel. (1996). The birth of Prolog. In *History of Programming Languages II* (pp. 331-367). New York, NY, USA: ACM.

R. G. Cowell. (1999). *Probabilistic Networks and Expert Systems*: Springer.

G. Cugola & H. A. Jacobsen. (2002). Using publish/subscribe middleware for mobile systems. *ACM SIGMOBILE Mobile Computing and Communications Review, 6*(4), 25-33.

O.-J. Dahl, B. Myhrhaug & K. Nygaard. (1968). *Some features of the SIMULA 67 language.* Conference Proceedings of the Second Conference on Applications of Simulations, New York, New York, United States.

M. Dastani, K. V. Hindriks, P. Novak & N. A. M. Tinnemeier. (2008). Combining Multiple Knowledge Representation Technologies into Agent Programming Languages. *Lecture Notes in Artificial Intelligence.*

C. J. Date. (2000). Twelve Rules for Business Rules.

C. J. Date. (2004). *An Introduction to Database Systems, Eight Edition.* Boston, San Francisco, New York: Pearson Education.

C. J. Date. (2007). *Logic and Databases - The Roots of Relational Theory*: Trafford.

T. Davenport, H. & L. Prusak. (2000). *Working Knowledge: How Organizations Manage What They Know*: Harvard Business School Press, Boston, MA.

F. D. Davis. (1989). Perceived Usefulness, Perceived Ease of Use, and User Acceptance of Information Technology. *MIS Quarterly, September 1989*, 319-333.

R. Davis, H. Shrobe & P. Szolovits. (1993). What is a Knowledge Representation. *AI Magazine, 14*(1), 17-33.

U. Dayal, E. N. Hanson & J. Widom. (1994). Active Database Systems. In W. Kim (Ed.), *Modern Database Systems: The Object Model, Interoperability and Beyond*. Reading/Massachusetts: Addison Wesley.

M. Dell'Erba, O. Fodor, W. Höpken & H. Werthner. (2005). Exploiting Semantic Web Technologies for Harmonizing E-Markets. *Information Technology & Tourism*, 201-220.

A. K. Dey. (2001). Understanding and Using Context. *Personal and Ubiquitous Computing, 5*(1), 4-7.

A. K. Dey & G. D. Abowd. (2000a). *CybreMinder: A Context-Aware System for Supporting Reminders.* Conference Proceedings of the Second International Symposium on Handheld and Ubiquitous Computing, Bristol, UK.

A. K. Dey & G. D. Abowd. (2000b). *Towards a Better Understanding of Context and Context Awareness.* Conference Proceedings of the Workshop on the What, Who, Where, When, and How of Context-Awareness, The Hague, The Netherlands.

A. K. Dey, G. D. Abowd & D. Salber. (2001). A Conceptual Framework and a Toolkit for Supporting the Rapid Prototyping of Context-Aware Applications. *Human-Computer Interaction, 16*(2-4), 97-166.

F. M. Donini, M. Lenzerini, D. Nardi & W. Nutt. (1991). *The Complexity of Concept Languages.* Conference Proceedings of the Knowledge Representation 91', Cambridge, Massachusetts, USA.

S. Dunstall, M. Horn, P. Kylbi, M. Krishnamoorthy, B. Owens, D. Sier & S. Thiebaux. (2003). An Automated Itinerary Planning System for Holiday Travel. *Information Technology & Tourism, 6*(3), 195-210.

A. Eberhart. (2002). *OntoAgent: A Platform for the Declarative Specification of Agents.* Conference Proceedings of the International Workshop on Rule Markup Languages for Business Rules on the Semantic Web. In conjunction with the 1rst International Semantic Web Conference (ISWC 2002), Chia, Sardinia, Italy.

Eclipse Foundation. (2008a). Rich Client Platform. Retrieved 2008-04-27, from http://www.eclipse.org/rcp/

Eclipse Foundation. (2008b). SWT: The Standard Widget Toolkit. Retrieved 2008-09-02, 2008, from http://www.eclipse.org/swt/

R. Elmasri & S. B. Navathe. (2006). *Fundamentals of database systems* (5th Edition ed.): Pearson Addison-Wesley.

Elsevier. (2005). elsevier TOC-ALERT. Retrieved 2008-09-01, 2008, from http://www.elsevier.de/blatt/d_journal_tocalert&_journal=805107

P. Eugster. (2007). Type-Based Publish/Subscribe: Concepts and Experiences. *ACM Transactions on Programming Languages and Systems (TOPLAS), 29*(1).

P. Eugster, P. Felber, R. Guerraoui & A.-M. Kermarrec. (2003). The many faces of publish/subscribe. *ACM Comput. Surv., 35*(2), 114-131.

E. A. Feigenbaum. (1992). Expert Systems: Principles and Practice.

D. Fensel, J. Hendler, H. Liebermann & W. Wahlster. (2003). *Spinning the Semantic Web*. Cambridge, Massachusetts
London, England: The MIT Press.

L. Fiege, F. C. Gärtner, O. Kasten & A. Zeidler. (2003a). *Supporting mobility in content-based publish/subscribe middleware.* Conference Proceedings of the International Middleware Conference (Middleware 2003), Rio de Janeiro, Brazil.

L. Fiege, G. Mühl & F. C. Gärtner. (2003b). Modular event-based systems. *The Knowledge Engineering Review, 14*(4), 359-388.

U. Forum. (2005). *Magic Mobile Future*. Technical Report, London.

M. Fowler. (2004). Inversion of Control Containers and the Dependency Injection pattern [Electronic Version]. Retrieved 2008-08-27 from http://martinfowler.com/articles/injection.html.

M. Frank. (1997). Pondering push technology. *DBMS, 10*(3), 8.

M. J. Franklin & S. B. Zdonik. (1998). *"Data In Your Face": Push Technology in Perspective.* Conference Proceedings of the ACM SIGMOD International Conference on Management of Data, Seattle, Washington, USA.

E. Friedman-Hill. (2003). *Jess in Action Rule-Based Systems in Java*. Greenwich, CT: Manning Publications Co. .

S. I. Gallant. (1993). *Neural Network Learning and Expert Systems*: MIT Press.

E. Gamma, R. Helm, R. Johnson & J. Vlissides. (1995). *Design Patterns: Elements of Reusable Object-Oriented Software*: Addison-Wesley Reading, MA.

S. Gatziu, A. Koschel, G. von Bültzingsloewen & H. Fritschi. (1998). Unbundling active functionality. *SIGMOD Record, 27*(1), 35-40.

D. Gawlick & S. Mishra. (2003). *Information sharing with the Oracle database.* Conference Proceedings of the 2nd international workshop on Distributed event-based systems, San Diego, California, USA.

N. H. Gehani, H. V. Jagadish & O. Shmueli. (1993). COMPOSE: A System For Composite Event Specification and Detection. In *Advanced Database Concepts, LNCS* (pp. 3-15): Springer-Verlag.

J. C. Giarratano & G. D. Riley. (2004). *Expert Systems: Principles and Programming* (Vol. 4. Edition): Course Technology.

I. P. Goldstein & R. B. Roberts. (1977). *NUDGE: A Knowledge-Based Scheduling Program.* Conference Proceedings of the Fifth IJCAI.

U. Gretzel & K. Wöber. (2004). *Intelligent Search Support: Building Search Term Associations for Tourism specific Search Engines.* Conference Proceedings of the Information and Communication Technologies in Tourism.

T. R. Gruber. (1993). A Translation Approach to Portable Ontology Specifications. *Knowledge Acquisition, An International Journal of Knowledge Acquisition for Knowledge Based Systems, 5*(2), 199-220.

T. Gu, H. Pung & D. Q. Zhang. (2004a). Toward an OSGI-based Infrastructure for Context-Aware Applications. *IEEE Pervasive Computing, 4*(2004), 66-74.

T. Gu, H. K. Pung & D. Q. Zhang. (2004b). *A Middleware for Building Context-Aware Mobile Services.* Conference Proceedings of the Vehicular Technology Conference, 2004, Milan, Italy.

T. Gu, X. H. Wang, H. K. Pung & D. Q. Zhang. (2004c). An Ontology-based Context Model in Intelligent Environments. *Proceedings of Communication Networks and Distributed Systems Modeling and Simulation Conference, 2004.*

J. F. J. Hair, Anderson, Tatham & Black. (2005). *Multivariate Data Analysis* (6th ed.): Prentice Hall.

T. Halpin. (2001). *Information Modeling and Relational Databases - From Conceptual Analysis to Logical Design*: Morgan Kaufmann.

E. N. Hanson & J. Widom. (1993). An Overview of production rules in database systems. *Knowledge Engineering Review, 8*(2), 121-143.

F. Hayes-Roth. (1985). Rule-based systems. *Communications of the ACM, 28*(9), 921-932.

H. Helbig. (2001). *Die Semantische Struktur Natürlicher Sprache: Wissensrepräsentation Mit MultiNet*: Springer.

M. Hellenschmidt & R. Wichert. (2007). Rule-Based Modeling of Inteligent Environment Behaviour. *Künstliche Intelligenz*(2/2007), 24-29.

K. Henricksen. (2003). *A Framework for Context-Aware Pervasive Computing Applications.* (Doctoral dissertation, The University of Queensland, 2003).

K. Henricksen & J. Indulska. (2004). *A Software Engineering Framework for Context-Aware Pervasive Computing.* Conference Proceedings of the 2nd IEEE Conference on Pervasive Computing and Communications (PerCom), Orlando, USA.

K. Henricksen & J. Indulska. (2006). Developing Context-Aware Pervasive Computing Applications: Models and Approach. *Journal of Pervasive and Mobile Computing, 2*(1), 37-64.

K. Henricksen, J. Indulska, T. McFadden & S. Balasubramaniam. (2005). Middleware for Distributed Context-Aware Systems. *Lecture Notes in Computer Science, 3760*, 846-863.

Hibernate. (2007). Hibernate Query Language. Retrieved 2008-03-04, 2008, from http://www.hibernate.org/hib_docs/reference/en/html/queryhql.html

Hibernate. (2008). Relational Persistence for Java and .NET. Retrieved 2008-10-12, from http://www.hibernate.org/

A. Hinze. (2003). *A-MEDIAS: Concept and Design of an Adaptive Integrating Event Notification Service.* (Doctoral dissertation, Freie Universität, Berlin, Germany, 2003).

A. Hinze & A. Voisard. (2003a). *Combining Event Notification Services and Location-Based Services In Tourism.* Technical Report, Berlin. Freie Universitaet Berlin.

A. Hinze & A. Voisard. (2003b). *Locations- and Time-Based Information Delivery in Tourism.* Conference Proceedings of the Advances in Spatial and Temporal Databases, 8th International Symposium, Santorini Island, Greece.

T. Hofer, W. Schwinger, M. Pichler, G. Leonhartsberger & J. Altmann. (2003). *Context-Awareness on Mobile Devices - the Hydrogen Approach.* Conference Proceedings of the 36th Annual Hawaii International Conference on System Sciences, Hawaii.

W. Höpken, M. Fuchs, M. Zanker, T. Beer, A. Eybl, S. Flores, S. Gordea, M. Jessenitschnig, T. Kerner, D. Linke, J. Rasinger & M. Schnabl. (2006). *etPlanner: An IT Framework for Comprehensive and Integrative Travel Guidance.* Conference Proceedings of the International Conference on Information Technology and Travel & Tourism (ENTER '06), Lausanne.

W. Höpken, M. Scheuringer, D. Linke, M. Fuchs & E. C. C. Austria. (2008). Context-based Adaptation of Ubiquitous Web Applications in Tourism. In *Information Technologies in Tourism 2008*: Springer.

E. M. Housman & E. D. Kaskela. (1970). State of the Art in Selective Dissemination of Information. *Engineering Writing and Speech, IEEE Transactions, 13*(2), 78-83.

M. Huth & M. Ryan. (2004). *Logic in Computer Science, Second Edition.* Cambridge: Cambridge University Press.

IBM TJ Watson Research Center. (2001). Gryphon: Publish/Subscribe over Public Networks.

IEEE Xplore. (2008). IEEE xplore release 2.5 alert. Retrieved 2008-09-01, 2008, from http://ieeexplore.ieee.org/xpl/tocalerts_signup.jsp

ilbi. (2008). intelligent local based information (ilbi) Retrieved 2008-07-30, 2008, from http://www.ilbi.eu/php/portal.php

J. Indulska & P. Sutton. (2003). *Location management in pervasive systems.* Conference Proceedings of the Australasian information security workshop conference on ACSW frontiers 2003, Adelaide, Australia.

P. Jackson. (1999). *Introduction to Expert Systems, 3rd ed.*: Addison Wesley.

D. Jannach. (2004). *Advisor Suite – A Knowledge-Based Sales Advisory System.* Conference Proceedings of the European Conference on Artificial Intelligence – PAIS, Valencia, Spain.

D. Jannach. (2006). *Finding Preferred Query Relaxations in Content-based Recommenders.* Conference Proceedings of the IEEE Intelligent Systems Conference IS'2006, Westminster, UK.

J. Jaynes. (1976). *The Origins of Consciousness in the Breakdown of the Bicameral Mind.* Princeton.

J. E. Kendall & K. E. Kendall. (1999). Information Delivery Systems: An Exploration of Web Pull and Push Technologies. *Communications of the AIS, 1*(4).

J. Kolodner. (1993). *Case-Based Reasoning*: Morgan Kaufmann Publishers Inc. San Francisco, CA, USA.

J. A. Konstan, J. Riedl, A. Borchers & J. L. Herlocker. (1998). Recommender Systems: A GroupLens Perspective. *Papers from the 1998 Workshop (AAAI Technical Report WS-98-08).* 60-64.

P. Kruchten. (1995). Architectural Blueprints - The "4+1" View Model of Software Architecture. *IEEE Software, 12*(6), 42--50.

P. Kruchten. (2003). *The Rational Unified Process: An Introduction*: Addison-Wesley Professional.

L. W. Lacy. (2005). *OWL: Representing Information Using the Web Ontology Language*: Trafford Publishing.

W. Lehner & W. Hümmer. (2001). The Revolution Ahead: Publish/Subscribe meets Database Systems. In W. Lehner (Ed.), *Advanced Techniques in Personalized Information Delivery. Arbeitsbericht des Instituts für Informatik, Friedrich-Alexander Universität Erlangen-Nürnberg.*

H. J. Levesque & R. J. Brachman. (1985). *A Fundamental Tradeoff in Knowledge Representation and Reasoning (Final Version)*: Morgan Kaufmann.

S. Li, Y. Lin, S. H. Son, J. A. Stankovic & Y. Wei. (2004). Event Detection Services Using Data Service Middleware in Distributed Sensor Networks. *Telecommunication Systems, 26*(2-4), 351-368.

S. H. Liao. (2005). Expert System Methodologies and Applications — A Decade Review from 1995 to 2004. *Expert Systems with Applications, 28*(1), 93-103.

R. K. Lindsay, B. G. Buchanan, E. A. Feigenbaum & J. Lederberg. (1980). *Applications of Artificial Intelligence for Organic Chemistry: The DENDRAL Project*: McGraw-Hill.

H. Liu & H.-A. Jacobsen. (2004). *A-ToPSS: A Publish/Subscribe System Supporting Imperfect Information Processing.* Conference Proceedings of the 30th International Conference on Very Large Databases (VLDB), Toronto, Canada.

D. Luckham. (2002). *The power of events: An Introduction to Complex Event Processing in Distributed Enterprise systems.* Amsterdam: Addison-Wesley Longman.

C. M. MacKenzie, K. Laskey, F. McCabe, P. F. Brown & R. Metz. (2006). Reference Model for Service Oriented Architecture 1.0 [Electronic Version]. Retrieved 2008-04-30 from http://docs.oasis-open.org/soa-rm/v1.0/soa-rm.html.

N. Marmasse & C. Schmandt. (2000). Location-Aware Information Delivery with ComMotion. *Lecture Notes in Computer Science, 1927*(2000), 361-370.

D. Marshall. (1999). Remote Procedure Calls (RPC) Retrieved 2008-09-02, 2008, from http://www.cs.cf.ac.uk/Dave/C/node33.html

W. May, J. J. Alferes & R. Amador. (2005a). *Active Rules in the Semantic Web: Dealing with Language Heterogeneity.* Conference Proceedings of the First International Conference on Rules and Rule Markup Languages for the Semantic Web (RuleML 2005), Galway, Ireland.

W. May, J. J. Alferes & R. Amador. (2005b). An Ontology-and Resources-Based Approach to Evolution and Reactivity in the Semantic Web. In *On the Move to Meaningful Internet Systems 2005: CoopIS, DOA, and ODBASE* (Vol. 3761, pp. 1553-1570): Springer Berlin/Heidelberg.

B. McBride. (2004). The Resource Description Framework (RDF) and its Vocabulary Description Language RDFS. In S. Staab & R. Studer (Eds.), *Handbook on Ontologies*. Karlsruhe: Springer.

D. McCarthy & U. Dayal. (1989). The architecture of an active database management system. *ACM SIGMOD Record, 18*(2), 215-224.

J. McCarthy. (1989). Artificial Intelligence, Logic and Formalizing Common Sense. In R. Thomason (Ed.), *Philosophical Logic and Artificial Intelligence* (pp. 161–190): Kluwer Academic.

J. McCarthy & P. Hayes. (1969). *Some philosophical problems from the standpoint of artificial intelligence* (Vol. 4): Wiley, New York.

D. L. McGuinness & F. van Harmelen. (2004). OWL Web Ontology Language Overview. Retrieved 10.11.2005, 2005, from http://www.w3.org/2004/OWL/

B. Meyer. (1997). *Object-Oriented Software Construction*: Prentice Hall Upper Saddle River, NJ.

M. Minsky. (1975). A Framework for Representing Knowledge. In P. Winston (Ed.), *The Psychology of Computer Vision* (pp. 211-280). New York, USA: McGraw-Hill.

M. Minsky. (1986). *The Society of Mind*: Simon & Schuster, Inc. New York, NY, USA.

J. M. V. Misker & J. R. Anderson. (2003). Combining Optimality Theory and a Cognitive Architecture. *Proceedings of the Fifth International Conference on Cognitive Modeling, Universitaetsverlag*, 165-170.

J. C. Mitchell. (2003). *Concepts in Programming Languages*. Cambridge: Cambridge University Press.

G. Mühl. (2002). *Large-Scale Content-Based publish subscribe systems*. (Doctoral dissertation, Technische Universität, Darmstadt, 2002).

G. Mühl, L. Fiege & P. R. Pietzuch. (2006). *Distributed Event-Based Systems*. Berlin, Heidelberg, New York: Springer.

C. Nikolopoulos. (1997). *Expert Systems - Introduction to First and Second Generation and Hybrid Knowledge Based Systems*. New York: CRC.

M. O'Grady & G. O'Hare. (2002). Accessing Cultural Tourist Information Via a Context-Sensitive Tourist Guide. *Information Technology & Tourism, 5*(1), 35-47.

C. K. Ogden & I. A. Richards. (1989). *The Meaning of Meaning: A Study of the Influence of Language Upon Thought and of the Science of Symbolism*: Harcourt.

B. Oki, M. Pfluegl, A. Siegel & D. Skeen. (1993). *The Information Bus: An Architecture for Extensible Distributed Systems*. Conference Proceedings of the 14th Symposium on Operating Systems Principles, Asheville, NC, USA.

OMG. (2004). Notification Service, version 1.1 [Electronic Version]. Retrieved 2008-08-20 from http://www.omg.org/technology/documents/formal/notification_service.htm.

OpenSymphony. (2008a). Quartz - CronTrigger [Electronic Version]. Retrieved 2008-08-27 from http://www.opensymphony.com/quartz/wikidocs/TutorialLesson6.html.

OpenSymphony. (2008b). Quartz - Quartz Overview [Electronic Version]. Retrieved 2008-06-10 from http://www.opensymphony.com/quartz/.

OSGi Alliance. (2008). OSGi™ - The Dynamic Module System for Java™ [Electronic Version]. Retrieved 2008-05-27 from http://www.osgi.org.

L. Palopoli & R. Torlone. (1997). Generalized Production Rules as a Basis for Integrating Active and Deductive Databases. *IEEE Transactions on Knowledge and Data Engineering, 9*(6), 848-862.

G. A. Papadopoulos & F. Arbab. (1998). Coordination models and languages. *The Enineering of Large Systems. Advances in Computers, vol. 46*, Academic Press, New York, NY.

G. Papamarkos, A. Poulovassilis & P. T. Wood. (2003). *Event-Condition-Action Rule Languages for the Semantic Web*. Paper presented at the Workshop on Semantic Web and Databases.

G. Papamarkos, A. Poulovassilis & P. T. Wood. (2004). *RDFTL: An Event-Condition-Action Language for RDF*. Conference Proceedings of the 3rd Hellenic Data Management Symposium (HDMS'04), Athens, Greece.

F. Pascal. (2006). Business Modeling for Database Design: A Foundation Framework for Data Management.

J. Pascoe. (1997). *The Stick-E Note Architecture: Extending the Interface Beyond the User*. Conference Proceedings of the International Conference on Intelligent User Interfaces, Orlando, Florida.

J. Pascoe. (1998). *Adding Generic Contextual Capabilities to Wearable Computers*. Conference Proceedings of the 2nd International Symposium on Wearable Computers (ISWC), Pittsburgh, USA.

A. Pashtan, R. Blattler, A. Heuser & P. Scheuermann. (2003). *CATIS: A Context-Aware Tourist Information System*. Paper presented at the IMC 2003 - 4th International Workshop of Mobile Computing.

L. Passani. (2008). wurfl. Retrieved 2008-09-26, 2008, from http://wurfl.sourceforge.net/

N. W. Paton & O. Díaz. (1999). Active Database Systems. *ACM Computing Surveys, 31*(1).

J. Pereira, F. Fabret, H. Jacobesen, F. Llirbat, R. Preotiuc-Prieto, K. Ross & D. Shasha. (2001). *Le subscribe: Publish and subscribe on the web at extreme speed*. Conference Proceedings of the ACM SIGMOD International Conference on Management of Data, Santa Barbara, CA, USA.

P. R. Pietzuch. (2004). Hermes: A Scalable Event-Based Middleware. *University of Cambridge PhD Thesis*.

P. R. Pietzuch, B. Shand & J. Bacon. (2004). Composite event detection as a generic middleware extension. *Network, IEEE, 18*(1), 44-55.

PostgreSQL Global Development Group. (2008). PostgreSQL. Retrieved 2008-03-10, 2008, from http://www.postgresql.org/

S. Powers. (2003). *Practical RDF*: O'Reilly.

S. Ramakrishnan & V. Dayal. (1998). The PointCast Network. *ACM SIGMOD Record, 27*(2), 520.

J. Rasinger, M. Fuchs & W. Höpken. (2007). Information search with mobile tourist guides: A survey of usage intention. *Information Technology & Tourism, 9*(3/4).

J. Rasinger, M. Fuchs, W. Höpken & T. Beer. (2008). Building a Mobile Tourist Guide based on Tourists' On-Site Information Needs. *Tourism Analysis*.

J. Rasinger, M. Fuchs, W. Höpken & M. Tuta. (2006). *A Customer based Approach to discover accepted Mobile Information Services in Tourism*. Conference Proceedings of the EyeforTravel, London.

F. Ricci, N. Mirzadeh, A. Venturini & H. Werthner. (2001). *Case-based Reasoning and Legacy Data Reuse for Web-based Recommendation Architectures*. Conference Proceedings of the Third International Conference on Information Integration and Web-based Applications and Services (IIWAS2001), Linz.

F. Ricci & H. Werthner. (2002). Case Base Querying for Travel Planning Recommendation. *Information Technology & Tourism, 4*, 215-226.

R. G. Ross. (2003). *Principles of the Business Rule Approach*: Addison-Wesley.

S. J. Russel & P. Norvig. (2003). *Atificial Intelligence: A modern approach*. Upper Saddle River: Prentice Hall Series in Artificial Intelligence.

N. Ryan, J. Pascoe & D. Morse. (1997). *Enhanced Reality Fieldwork: the Context Aware Archaeological Assistant*.

G. Salton. (1968). *Automatic Information Organization and Retrieval*: McGraw Hill Text.

M. Schacher & P. Grässle. (2006). *Agile Unternehmen durch Business Rules*. Berlin, Heidelberg. Germany: Springer-Verlag.

J. B. Schafer, J. Konstan & J. Riedi. (1999). *Recommender Systems in E-Commerce*. Conference Proceedings of the First ACM Conference on Electronic Commerce, Denver, CO, USA.

J. B. Schafer, J. A. Konstan & J. Riedl. (2001). E-Commerce Recommendation Applications. *Data Mining and Knowledge Discovery, 5*(1), 115-153.

B. N. Schilit, N. Adams & R. Want. (1994). *Context-Aware Computing Applications*. Conference Proceedings of the IEEE Workshop on Mobile Computing Systems and Applications.

B. N. Schilit & M. M. Theimer. (1994). Disseminating Active Map Information to Mobile Hosts. *IEEE Network, 8*, 22-32.

A. Schmidt, M. Beigl & H.-W. Gellersen. (1999). *There is more to context than location*. Conference Proceedings of the Intl. Workshop on Interactive Applications of Mobile Computing (IMC98), Rostock, Germany.

W. Schwinger, C. Grün, B. Pröll, W. Retschitzegger & A. Schauerhuber. (2005). *Context-Awareness in Mobile Tourism Guides–A Comprehensive Survey*. Technical Report, Linz/Austria. Johannes Kepler University.

W. Schwinger, C. Grün, B. Pröll, W. Retschitzegger & H. Werthner. (2006). *Pinpointing Tourism Information onto Mobile Maps–A Light-Weight Approach*. Conference Proceedings of the ENTER - International Conference on Information Technology and Travel & Tourism.

Sengaro GmbH. (2009). mobeedo, The Open Multi-Purpose Information System for the Mobile Age. 2009-02-10, from http://www.mobeedo.com/

M. Shanahan. (1999). The Event Calculus Explained In *Artificial Intelligence Today: Recent Trends and Developments (Lecture Notes in Computer Science)* (Vol. 1600): Springer Berlin / Heidelberg.

Q. Z. Sheng & B. Benatallah. (2005). *ContextUML: A UML-Based Modeling Language for Model-Driven Development of Context-Aware Web Services*. Conference Proceedings of the The 4th International Conference on Mobile Business (ICMB'05), Sydney, Australia.

A. Singh & M. Conway. (2006). *Survey of Context aware frameworks - Analysis and Criticism*. Technical Report, Chapel Hill, USA. University of North Carolina.

sms.at. (2008). sms.at. Retrieved 2008-11-22, from http://www.sms.at/

B. Smyth. (2007). Case-Based Recommendation. In P. Brusilovsky, A. Kobsa & W. Neydl (Eds.), *The Adaptive Web: Methods and Strategies of Web Personalization* (pp. 342-376): Springer, Heidelberg, Germany.

J. F. Sowa. (2000). *Knowledge Representation: Logical, Philosophical, and Computational Foundations*. Pacific Grove, CA: Brooks Cole Publishing.

Spring Source. (2006, 2008-08-27). Spring Framework. from http://www.springframework.org/

Springer. (2008). SpringerLink Alerts. Retrieved 2008-09-01, 2008, from http://www.springerlink.com

S. Staab & R. Studer. (2004). *Handbook on Ontologies*. Karlsruhe: Springer.

S. Staab & H. Werthner. (2002). Intelligent Systems for Tourism. *IEEE Intelligent Systems, November/December*, 53-66.

T. Strang. (2003). *Service-Interoperabilität in Ubiquitous Computing Umgebungen*. (Doctoral dissertation, Ludwig-Maximilians-Universität München, München, 2003).

T. Strang & C. Linnhoff-Popien. (2004). *A Context Modeling Survey*. Conference Proceedings of the UbiComp 2004 - The Sixth International Conference on Ubiquitous Computing, Nottingham/England.

R. Strom, G. Banavar, T. Chandra, M. Kaplan, K. Miller, B. Mukherjee, D. Sturman & M. Ward. (1998). *Gryphon: An Information Flow Based Approach to Message Brokering*. Conference Proceedings of the ISSRE International Symposium on Software Reliability Engineering, Paderborn, Germany.

K. J. Sullivan & D. Notkin. (1990). *Reconciling Environment Integration and Component Independence*. Conference Proceedings of the 4th ACM SIGSOFT Symposium on Sotware Development Environments.

K. J. Sullivan & D. Notkin. (1992). Reconciling Environment Integration and Scftware Evolution. *ACM Transactions of Software Engineering and Methodology, 1*(3), 229-269.

Sun Microsystems Inc. (2002). Java Messaging Service, Version 1.1.

Sun Microsystems Inc. (2008a). Getting Started with Swing. Retrieved 2008-09-02, 2008, from http://java.sun.com/docs/books/tutorial/uiswing/start/index.html

Sun Microsystems Inc. (2008b). Java Remote Method Invocation - Distributed Computing for Java. Retrieved 2008-09-02, 2008, from http://java.sun.com/javase/technologies/core/basic/rmi/whitepaper/index.jsp

tisCOVER. (2008). tisCOVER.com, more than travel. Retrieved 2008-11-28, from http://www.tiscover.com/

J. D. Ullman. (1988). *Principles of Database And Knowledge - Base Systems* (Vol. 1): Computer Science Press.

UserLand Software. (2003). Simple cross-platform distributed computing, based on the standards of the Internet. Retrieved 2008-09-02, 2008, from http://www.xmlrpc.com/

J. J. van Griethuysen. (1982). *Concepts and Terminology for the Conceptual Schema and the Information Base*: International Organization for Standardization.

H. van Kranenburg, M. S. Bargh, S. Iacob & A. Peddemors. (2006). A Context Management Framework for Supporting Context-Aware Distributed Applications. *IEEE Communications Magazine, 44*(8), 67-74.

M. van Setten, S. Pokraev & J. Koolwaaij. (2004). Context-Aware Recommendations in the Mobile Tourist Application COMPASS. In *Lecture Notes in Computer Science*: Springer, Berlin/Heidelberg, Germany.

Velocity. (2007). Velocity Template Engine. Retrieved 2008-03-10, 2008, from http://velocity.apache.org/

V. Venkatesh, M. Morris, G. B. Davis & F. D. Davis. (2003). User Acceptance of Information Technology: Toward a Unified View. *MIS Quarterly, 27*(3), 425-478.

C. Vogt, R. Walter, J. Rasinger & G. Specht. (2007). *InfoArea - an Open Multi-Purpose Information System for the Mobile Age*. Conference Proceedings of the International Conference on Advances in Mobile Computing and Multimedia (MoMM2007), Jakarta, Indonesia.

W3C. (1999). XML Path Language (XPath). Retrieved 2008-09-26, from http://www.w3.org/TR/xpath

W3C. (2007). XQuery 1.0: An XML Query Language. Retrieved 2008-02-05, from http://www.w3.org/TR/xquery/

F. G. Wachter. (2008). Konzeption und Implementierung eines Editors für die Erstellung und Pflege von E-C-A Regeln (Bachelor Thesis, Institute of Computer Science, Leopold-Franzens-University of Innsbruck, Austria, 2008).

R. Want, A. Hopper, V. Falcao & J. Gibbons. (1992). The Active Badge Location System. *ACM Transactions on Information Systems, 10*(1), 91-102.

I. Watson & F. Marir. (1994). Case-Based Reasoning: A Review. *The Knowledge Engineering Review, 9*(4), 327-354.

M. Weiser. (1991). The Computer for the 21st Century. *Scientific American, Sept. 1991*, 94-104.

H. Werthner. (2008). Lecture e-commerce 2008 Vienna University of Technology; based on Presentation of J. Kim, at "Recommenders06 - Summer School on The Present and Future of Recommender Systems", Bilbao. Spain, 2006.

H. Werthner & S. Klein. (1999). *Information Technology and Tourism: A Challenging Relationship*. Vienna, New York, Test: Springer.

J. Widom & S. Ceri. (1996). *Active Database Systems: Triggers and Rules for Advanced Database Processing*: Morgan Kaufmann.

L. Wunderlich. (2006). *Java Rules Engines. Entwicklung von regelbasierten Systemen*: entwickler.press.

XQueue GmbH. (2008). XQueue E-Mail Marketing Platform. Retrieved 2008-11-26, from http://www.xqueue.com

T. W. Yan & H. Garcia-Molina. (1994). *Distributed selective dissemination of information*. Paper presented at the PDIS International Conference on Parallel and Distributed Information Systems.

T. W. Yan & H. Garcia-Molina. (1995). *SIFT - A Tool for Wide-Area Information Dissemination*. Conference Proceedings of the USENIX Technical Conference on UNIX and Advanced Computing Systems, New Orleans, LA, USA.

J. Yen, R. Neches & R. MacGregor. (1989). *Classification-Based Programming: A Deep Integration of Frames and Rules*. Technical Report, Marina del Rey / California. University of Southern California Marina Del Rey Information Science Institute.

ZAMG. (2008). Central Institute for Meteorology and Geodynamics. Retrieved 2008-11-29, from http://www.zamg.ac.at

M. Zanker, S. Gordea, M. Jessenitschnig & M. Schnabl. (2006). *A Hybrid Similarity Concept for Browsing Semistructured Product Items*. Conference Proceedings of the 7th International Conference on Electronic Commerce and Web Technologies - EC-Web '06.

M. Zanker, W. Höpken, M. Fuchs, M. Aschinger, T. Beer, M. Jessenitschnig, D. Linke & J. Rasinger. (2008). *innsbruck.mobile: A Collaborative Tourist Recommender Based on Multiple Evidence*. Technical Report, Innsbruck, Austria. eTourism Competence Center Austria, Innsbruck, Austria / University Klagenfurt, Klagenfurt, Austria.

M. Zanker & M. Jessenitschnig. (2008). Case-studies on Exploiting Explicit Customer Requirements in Recommender Systems, User Modeling and User-Adapted Interaction. In A. Tuzhilin & B. Mobasher (Eds.), *The Journal of Personalization Research: Special issue on Data Mining for Personalization, to appear 2008/09*.

A. Zeidler. (2004). *A Distributed Publish/Subscribe Notification Service for Pervasive Environments*. (Doctoral dissertation, Technical University, Darmstadt, 2004).

C. Zins. (2008). What is the meaning of "data", "information", and "knowledge"? [Electronic Version]. Retrieved 2008-05-03 from http://www.success.co.il/is/dik.html.

VDM Verlagsservicegesellschaft mbH

Die VDM Verlagsservicegesellschaft sucht für wissenschaftliche Verlage abgeschlossene und herausragende

Dissertationen, Habilitationen, Diplomarbeiten, Master Theses, Magisterarbeiten usw.

für die kostenlose Publikation als Fachbuch.

Sie verfügen über eine Arbeit, die hohen inhaltlichen und formalen Ansprüchen genügt, und haben Interesse an einer honorarvergüteten Publikation?

Dann senden Sie bitte erste Informationen über sich und Ihre Arbeit per Email an *info@vdm-vsg.de*.

Sie erhalten kurzfristig unser Feedback!

VDM Verlagsservicegesellschaft mbH
Dudweiler Landstr. 99
D - 66123 Saarbrücken

Telefon +49 681 3720 174
Fax +49 681 3720 1749

www.vdm-vsg.de

Die VDM Verlagsservicegesellschaft mbH vertritt

Printed by Books on Demand GmbH, Norderstedt / Germany